(ADVANCE REVIEW COPY)

Everything That Remains

a memoir by The Minimalists

JOSHUA FIELDS MILLBURN
with interruptions by Ryan Nicodemus

Asymmetrical Press
Missoula, Montana

PRAISE FOR THE MINIMALISTS

"Like Henry David Thoreau, but with Wi-Fi."
—*Boston Globe*

"Paring down, branching out."
—*Chicago Tribune*

"A better life, by having fewer possessions."
—*Seattle Times*

"Minimalism has brought happiness to [these] two former executives."
—*Vancouver Sun*

"They just might give you a hug."
—*Dayton Daily News*

"Regaining control by limiting consumption and living more meaningful lives."
—*Forbes*

"The best way to find happiness is to get rid of almost everything."
—*CBS This Morning*

"Perhaps it's a good time to sit back and look at how we can all live with less."
—*USA Today*

"Less has become so much more.... Let's call it minimalism+."
—*Elle Canada*

"Minimalists make the most of living with very little."
—*Chicago Sun-Times*

"The path to a richer, if less cluttered, life."
—*Globe & Mail*

"Frugality so satisfying."
—*Wall Street Journal*

"Passionate about helping people."
—*San Francisco Chronicle*

"Minimalists maximize lives by letting go selectively."
—*Austin American-Statesman*

"Meet Generation M."
—*Toronto Star*

"Living a better life…with less stuff."
—*National Post*

"By getting rid of everything they don't need, [The Minimalists] concentrate on the things in life that are truly important to them."
—*Missoulian*

"Two former corporate professionals who willingly walked away from handsome salaries and material-laden lifestyles at the end of their 20s, to live 'a meaningful life' with less stuff."
—*Business Insider*

"Free up more time for your family and ultimately simplify your life."
—*Colorado Parent Magazine*

"Eliminating the unnecessary stuff that clutters the mind."
—*Mint.com*

"How to have it all, with less."
—*Huffington Post*

"Less is more, even during the holidays."
—*San Francisco Examiner*

"Helping us end our obsession with stuff."
—*LA Weekly*

BOOKS BY THE MINIMALISTS

NONFICTION
Minimalism: Live a Meaningful Life
Everything That Remains

ESSAY COLLECTIONS
A Day in the Life of a Minimalist
Essential Essays
Simplicity

FICTION (by JFM)
Falling While Sitting Down: Stories
Days After the Crash: A Novella
As a Decade Fades: A Novel

ABOUT THE MINIMALISTS

Joshua Fields Millburn and Ryan Nicodemus have garnered an audience of more than 2 million readers at *TheMinimalists.com*. They are the bestselling authors of five nonfiction and three fiction books. Both born in 1981, they live in Montana by way of Dayton, Ohio.

Published by Asymmetrical Press.

© 2014 by Joshua Fields Millburn and Ryan Nicodemus. All rights reserved.

Love people, use things. The opposite doesn't work.

Feel free to take pieces of this book and replicate them online or in print, but please link back to theminimalists.com. If you want to use more than a few paragraphs, that's great—please email press@theminimalists.com. If you illegally downloaded this book or stole a paperback version from the library or something, then shame on you! But please at least share your lifted copy with a friend or an enemy or anyone who might benefit from its words.

Library of Congress Cataloging-in-Publication Data
Everything that remains / Millburn, Nicodemus — advance review copy
ARC ISBN: 978-1-938793-29-5
WC: 64,224
1. Minimalism. 2. Happiness. 3. The Minimalists.
4. Simplicity. 5. Consumerism. 6. Self-help. 7. Careers.

Photography by Adam Dressler
Cover design by Dave LaTulippe
PR by Sarah Miniaci
Typeset in Garamond
Formatted in beautiful Montana
Printed in the U.S.A.

Author info:
Publisher: asymmetrical.co/jfm
Fiction: joshuafieldsmillburn.com
Essays: theminimalists.com
Email: press@theminimalists.com
Twitter: @theminimalists

ASYM METR ICAL

For Colin

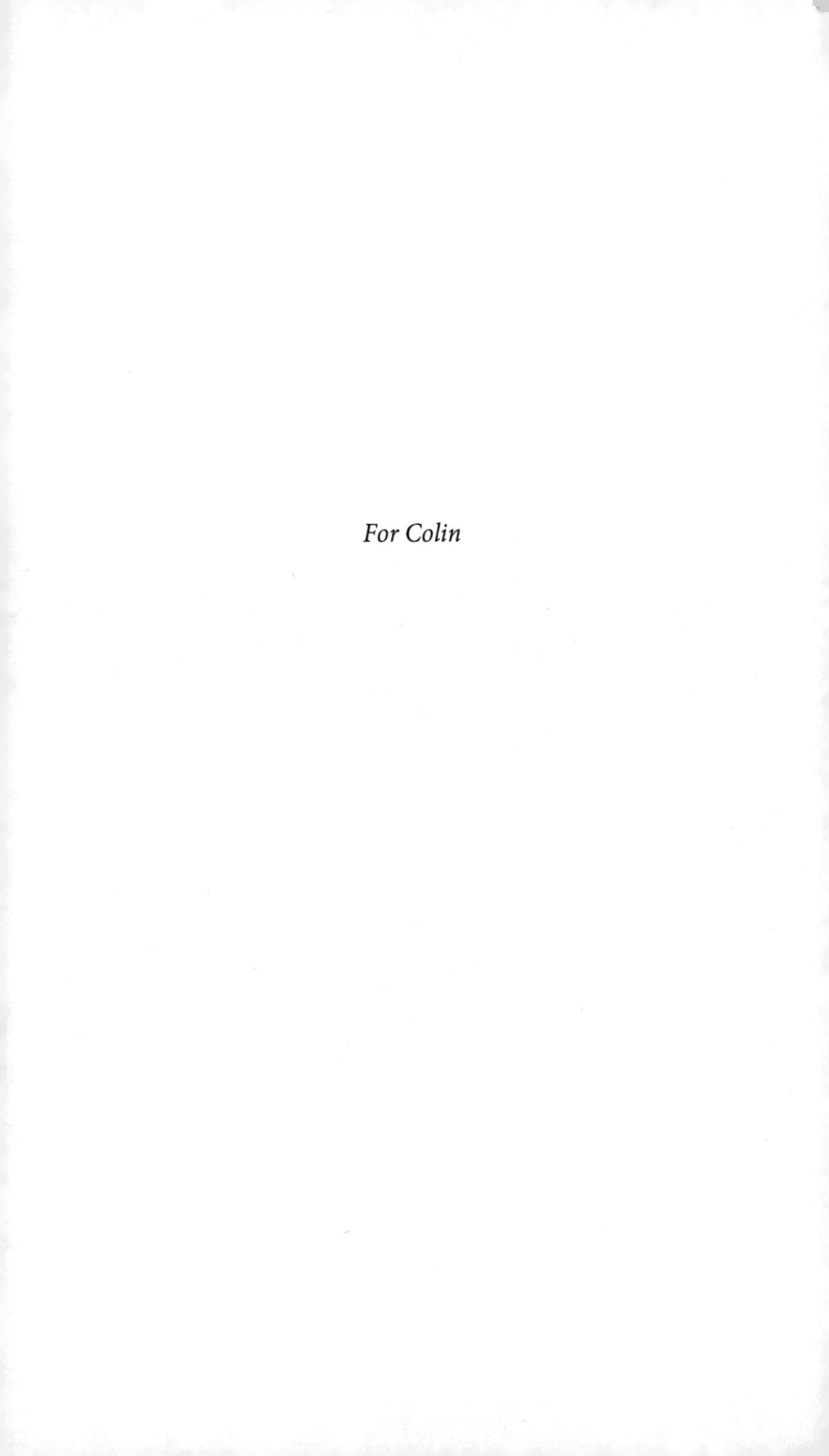

So yo then man what's your story?

—DAVID FOSTER WALLACE,
Infinite Jest

CONTENTS

A Note for the Reader 1

PART ONE | EVERYTHING

1. Fluorescent Ghosts (December 2008) 5

2. Stray Age (October 2009) 27

3. Blood on the Flag (November 2009) 35

4. Open Windows (December 2009) 45

5. Strong Moves Slow (June 2010) 67

6. The Sound of Minimalism (November 2010) 85

7. Clarity (December 2010) 109

PART TWO | REMAINS

8. A Well-Curated Life (September 2011) 127

9. Harvest Moon (October 2011) 153

10. Thoreau & the Unabomber (October 2012) 159

11. Beautiful Accidents (December 2012) 175

12. Rearviews & Windshields (March 2013) 189

Endnotes by Ryan Nicodemus 205

Everything That Remains

A Brief Note for the Reader

THIS BOOK is a work of nonfiction. Sort of. You see, all characters and entities herein really are real, and all the events actually did happen, but sometimes we had to make stuff up (e.g., specific dialogue, precise dates, the various colors of the sky).

Structured as a book-length, five-year conversation between its two authors, *Everything That Remains* is written as a first-person narrative by me (Joshua Fields Millburn) with intentional interruptions—comments, interjections, and smart-alecky remarks—from Ryan Nicodemus. This structure is somewhat mimetic of our in-person interactions (i.e., we like to interrupt each other—a lot). In the book, however, Ryan's interruptions take place in the form of endnotes.[1] These endnotes can be read when each interruption occurs or at the end of the book. As with everything in life, you get to choose.

It's worth noting that a handful of names—persons and corporations—were changed to avoid pissing off certain folks.[2] We also took occasional creative liberties to aid the flow and continuity of the book, which was attenuated (necessarily) from more than a thousand pages at its bloated nadir to its current slender tome. And it's almost certain that Ryan and I misremembered or couldn't agree on some people/events, and yet these misremembrances are, in a weird way, still *true*. After all, truth is perspectival, isn't it?

For want of a better descriptor, we decided to call this book a *memoir*. Trust me, I realize how pretentious it sounds to've written a memoir at thirty-two. But it's not really a memoir—more like a bunch of life lessons explored in a narrative format, which allowed Ryan and me to flesh out many of the topics we touch upon at our website, *TheMinimalists.com*, expanding on those topics by way of storytelling and conversation.[3] Besides, *autobiography* sounded too stiff and stilted, a title reserved for more important folk: presidents and tycoons and child actors with drug problems. If you hate the whole idea of calling this thing a memoir, then please feel free to call it something else. Call it a prescriptive-nonfiction novel. Call it a personal history. Call it a recipe book for a more meaningful life. Call it whatever you want. I won't mind.

—JFM

PART ONE || Everything

1 || Fluorescent Ghosts

DECEMBER 2008

Our identities are shaped by the costumes we wear. I am seated in a cramped conference room, surrounded by ghosts in shirtsleeves and pleated trousers. There are thirty-five, maybe forty, people here. Middle managers, the lot of us. Mostly Caucasian, mostly male, all oozing apathy. The group's median complexion is that of an agoraphobe.

A Microsoft Excel spreadsheet is projected onto an oversized canvas pulled from the ceiling at the front of the room. The canvas is flimsy and cracked and is a shade of off-white that suggests it's a relic from a time when employees were allowed to smoke indoors. The rest of the room is aggressively white: the walls are white, the ceiling is white, the people are white, as if all cut from the same materials. Well, everyone except Stan, seated at the back of the room. Cincinnati's population is forty-five percent black, but Stan is part of our company's single-digit percentage. His comments, rarely solicited by executives, are oft-dismissed with a nod and a pained smile. Although he's the size of an NFL linebacker, Stan is a paragon of kindness. But that doesn't stop me from secretly hoping that one day he will get fed up with the patronizing grins and make it his duty to reformat one of the bosses' fish-eyed faces.

You can't miss the enormous Broadspan logo on the wall behind us, a rapacious-looking line-drawn eagle, soaring, its wings outstretched, clutching the company's side-by-side vowels in its talons. "Right Here, Right Now," our occult tag line, is typeset below the logo in Helvetica Bold. If you say "Right Here, Right Now" repeatedly, it begins to take on a sort of metaphysical edge, a profound truism the skinny-tie guys in marketing didn't intend.

The end of another year is approaching. This is the final Monday Sales Meeting of the year. We are currently landlocked in the middle of the eleventh floor. Not a single beam of natural light can be seen from my vantage point, seated between my boss and my boss's boss, both of whom have Irish surnames and are nearly indistinguishable from one another. The air stinks of industrial-strength cleaning supplies and years of resentment. Every seat at the large Formica conference table is full, so a handful of latecomers are forced to stand, congregating toward the back of the room as if waiting to give confession. The table is littered with printed spreadsheets and half-empty Starbucks cups. Someone behind me yawns, which triggers several more yawns among the crowd. Boredom is contagious.

The projected spreadsheet is out of focus, so we're all staring forward, squinting, attempting to find something meaningful in the blur of numbers. The projector emits a drone of white noise that everyone pretends to ignore. But I can't ignore it. How could you? That incessant hum controls the atmosphere around us, holding hostage all other sounds. The overhead lights are partially switched off. Everyone is baptized in half-light, a hideous fluorescent glow that makes us all appear vaguely ill. There's another yawn across the table. And then another. A man with pudgy red cheeks sniffs twice and then wipes his nose on his cuff.

Ryan Nicodemus, my best friend of twenty years, the only man not wearing a tie, walks into the meeting wielding a massive coffee cup and a jutting jawline that carries an apologetic grin and a couple days' worth of dark stubble. He's swarthy and confident and very late.[4]

My boss (or is it his boss?) asks me a question that I don't realize is directed at me until I hear my name, "...so how do you explain the decline in attach rates this week, Millie?" Half my coworkers call me Millie, which seems endearing half the time, and patronizing the other half, depending on the person and their cadence. I look to my right and then my left. Both men are fixed on the glowing grid at the front of the room, their faces red with early-onset rosacea, a condition that makes them appear perpetually angry or embarrassed or somehow both at the same time. The spreadsheet, dull and cloudy, is color-coded green and red, apropos since it's three days till Christmas. The color scheme is inadvertent, though; it's always the same, every meeting, no matter the time of year: green is good, red is bad. Red dominates the blur today.

I look at the numbers and try to affect what I hope is a sufficiently displeased look, followed by one of my dozen or so standard laconic answers, some jargon about marketing-spend and GRPs and TPRs and a few other acronyms that are supposed to make me look like I have a well-informed grasp on the situation. Half the room nods sympathetically to the rhythm of my gnomic reasoning. The bosses seem pleased with my explanation. I pretend to jot a couple notes on my yellow legal pad, something "actionable." Ryan, now standing at the side of the room, just shakes his head at my line of bullshit. The projector is still thrumming, becoming more and more pronounced with each passing moment. HHHMMMMM.[5] The bosses move on to the next excuse baron.

At age twenty-seven, I'm the youngest director in my company's hundred and forty year history. For a while I thought this was impressive. You know, an admirable title to throw around when someone asks, as we invariably do, that most pernicious of questions: "What do you do?" To which I could respond with an air of accomplished pride: "I'm the director of operations for a hundred and fifty retail stores."

Fancy, right? Well, not exactly. You see, this is all pretty much one big accident. In more ways than one, my entire life has been an accident, so it's difficult to figure out exactly how I got Right Here, Right Now.

The accident started on June 29, 1981, at 2:39 p.m. in Dayton, Ohio, a bluecollar, rustbelt, car-manufacturing city. Brought into this world at the tail-end of Generation X, the self-centered Me Generation, I was born to a forty-two-year-old bipolar father and a thirty-six-year-old alcoholic mother. Ours was the blueprint of a dysfunctional family.[6] Of course that was before *dysfunctional* was in vogue.

Lowell, my broad-shouldered, silver-haired father, suffered from schizophrenia and had persistent, elaborate relationships with people who did not exist in the physical world. People who conspired against him to ruin his life. He was taller than most tall men, large in an ex-football player kind of way—three times the size of my mother, Chloe. Chloe was prettier than he was handsome. Together they were two wasted bodies of flesh, wallowing in their shared torment.

My first childhood memory is of the three of us in our livingroom on Green Street, me on the couch, my father's face hypertonic and expressionless as he extinguished a cigarette on Mom's bare chest, just below her clavicle. (A quarter-century later, my wife complains about my still lingering nightmares, my middle-of-the-night limb spasms and shrieking.) Mom finally left Lowell a year later; she started drinking more heavily around the same time. I was three.

I saw Lowell one other time, at Christmas when I was seven. Years later I found his death certificate; it noted advanced-stage alcoholic cardiomyopathy as the cause of his heart's failure. My only memory of his funeral is of Mom struggling with a broken umbrella at the burial ceremony underneath a pessimistic sky, the top spring failing to hold the umbrella's runner in place, causing the umbrella to collapse in on itself. I don't remember the six-hour drive to Chicago for the funeral. Nor do I remember the return trip. The downpour at the gravesite was torrential and unforgiving.

For much of my preadolescence I thought money came in two colors: green and white. Mom sometimes sold our white bills at a two-to-one ratio—fifty cents on the dollar—because she could purchase alcohol with only the green bills. Not once did I see any of the government-mandated nutritional pamphlets that were delivered with the white bills at the beginning of each month.

Mom earned minimum wage whenever she was able to hold a full-time job, but she was unable to for any appreciable period of time, because when she drank she went on benders in which she stayed shut in, in our one-bedroom duplex apartment, for days at a time, often not eating, just drinking heavily and chain-smoking Salem Lights from a green soft pack, stumbling and falling and ensconcing herself on the ash-daubed couch.

Red wine was Mom's preferred drink, though she settled for

tall cans of Milwaukee's Best—or whatever beer was least expensive that week—when she could not afford the bottom-shelf wines at the liquor store seven tedious blocks from our apartment. The store's owner sometimes allowed Mom to purchase beer or wine on store credit. The walk to the store was always fueled with buzz-filled exhilaration and anticipation, both of which placed a heavy fog over her shame, but the walk back was composed of a nervous expectancy, much like a child returning from the supermarket with a newly purchased toy, usually removing the toy's complicated packaging and playing with it in the car before making it halfway home. Similarly, Mom couldn't wait to unpackage her brown paper bag on the way home—*just one beer*, she'd justify to herself, to no one at all—and so the last three blocks were the hardest part of her trek home from the store, at times resulting in her halting to rest on one of several benches. Although if she stopped to rest, she almost assuredly had another beer—*just one more to take the edge off*—and on numerous occasions someone would find the ninety-pound woman drunk and asleep on a bench just a few blocks from her home, blanketed in erratic streetlight, a brown paper bag in her clutch.

Mom would return to our humid apartment, which smelled faintly of urine and empty beer cans and stale cigarette smoke—I can still smell it now—and when she was too drunk to venture into the kitchen, Mom's *modus operandi* was to hide her empty beer cans under the front flap at the base of the couch. Sometimes she was unable to make it to the bathroom on her own. The couch cushions had been flipped dozens of times. Cockroaches scattered every time I turned on a light. They appeared to come from the nextdoor neighbor's apartment. The neighbor was a kind and lonely man, a World War II veteran in his mid-seventies who seemed to own three or four apartments' worth of possessions and who didn't mind the bugs, perhaps because he had seen far worse, or maybe because they kept him company.

"Love thy neighbor" was the Matthew 22 scripture Mom muttered every time she killed a roach with her house slipper. Although when she drank, the scripture often morphed into "Fuck thy neighbor," and throughout most of my childhood I thought they were two different biblical passages, a sort of Old Testament vs. New Testament contradiction. Mom was a devout Catholic. She prayed daily, several times a day in fact, Rosary beads dangling, praying until her right thumb and nicotine-stained forefinger formed calluses, rotating through the string of beads, mouthing the same old Our Fathers and Hail Marys and even AA's Serenity Prayer, asking God to please take this from her, to please cure her of her disease, her DIS-EASE, please God please. But prayer after prayer, Serenity was a no-show. To my prepubescent self, God seemed to be either malevolent or impotent or maybe even both, if He existed at all.

I'd have to remove my shoes to count how many times our electricity got shut off on Warren Street,[7] which happened far more frequently at our apartment than at the neighbor's apartment. And when the lights went out in winter, and it was too cold to stay inside, Mom and I had special "sleepovers" at various men's houses. One of these men—a large man who wore a tie, which seemed unusual (none of the men who lived in our neighborhood wore ties other than on Sundays)—was later convicted of several counts of child molestation.

Mom regularly slept the afternoons away while I played G.I. Joe with a meager collection of action figures, carefully placing each figure back into plastic bins in an organized and methodical way whenever I was done, controlling the only thing I could control in my disorderly world, systematically separating the good guys into one bin and the bad guys into another bin and their weapons into yet a third bin (and every so often a few of the men switched sides from bad to good and vice versa).[8]

Grocery bags would sometimes materialize at our doorstep next to the gap where the three missing wooden planks used to be on the weather-stained, deteriorating porch. Mom said she had prayed to St. Anthony and that he had found us food. There were extended periods of time when I subsisted on St. Anthony's peanutbutter and white bread and packaged sugary foods like Pop-Tarts and Fruit Roll-Ups.

I fell off that same porch when I was seven. A rotted wood plank gave way under the weight of my pudgy preadolescent body, launching me face-first toward the sidewalk four feet below. There was blood and crying and a strange kind of dual panic: panic about the blood flowing from my busted chin, staining my clothes crimson; panic about Mom, who remained immobile on the couch when I ran inside the house screaming, arms flailing, unsure of what to do. The lonely walk to the emergency room was just over two miles. You can still see the scars from that fall today.

Each day after elementary school I would walk home to an empty house while Mom worked a second-shift job, or I'd come home and open the door and find Mom passed out on the couch, a cigarette still burning in the ashtray, an inch-and-a-half of undisturbed ash burnt down to almost the filter. It's like she misunderstood the term *stay-at-home mom*. My first-grade teacher referred to me on more than one occasion as a "latchkey kid," but I didn't know what that meant. I made friends with various elements of certain fringe social blocs, but never attempted to adapt to their tenets or fully integrate into any one particular group. I moved through junior high on this fringe, and by the time I hit puberty, and then high school, nearly all my friends were kids from the neighborhood, juvenile delinquents and drug dealers, all my age or a few years older. There was Jerome and Patch and Jamar, Judton and Mook and Pacho, J-9 and BLR and Big Will, most of whom would end up in prison before any of us turned twenty. Ryan didn't come around much during those years; his father wouldn't let him, so I was pretty much the only white kid in the bunch.

By age fourteen, I carried all the responsibilities of an adult, unconcerned with curfew, spending my evenings and weekends washing dishes for four dollars an hour at a local chain restaurant that seemed to cater only to geriatrics. On my sixteenth birthday, Mom surprised me with the gift of sobriety and an electric typewriter, the latter of which came from a pawn shop on the other side of town. (I was uncertain where the sobriety came from.)

At first, I thought of it as one of the many periods in which Mom would stop drinking for an extended period of time—she had stopped drinking for several consecutive months in the past—and then I thought I'd eventually return home late one night and find her once again off the wagon. But this time was different. This time Mom kept her seat on the wagon. It was unclear what triggered this newfound vigor for a life of temperance, and it was hard to swallow after watching her struggle for so many years. And yet every night when I returned home, I tentatively placed the key in the lock and cringed when I opened the door, fully expecting to see Mom sprawled out on the couch, semi-conscious with an inch-and-a-half of ash dangling from the tip of a burning cigarette. Every time I came home, though, she was awake and friendly and productive, an abstemious new woman. Within a few months Mom found a better-than-minimum-wage job at a local attorney's office, and we moved to a slightly nicer apartment without cockroaches, a cul-de-sac neighborhood on the other side of town. I even transitioned from white bread and Pop-Tarts to hearty, home-cooked meals. But every day I opened that door, the feeling never changed, and not knowing whether she was going to return to drinking was in many ways worse than coming home to her drunk and passed out. It was a different kind of hell knowing that any day she could relapse, because that was all I knew; that was what she was supposed to do, what was normal.

I moved out of Mom's home the day I turned eighteen, toting a large duffle bag, my electric typewriter, and a decade of future regrets.

I was convinced that if I got a job and made enough money, I could circumvent Mom's path; I could somehow achieve happiness.[9] So I spent my twenties traversing the corporate ladder. Fresh out of high school, I skipped the college route and found an entry-level sales job with Broadspan, a large telecom company that "let" me work six, sometimes seven, days a week, ten to twelve hours a day. I wasn't great at it, but I learned how to get by—and then how to get better.

I bought a big-screen TV, a surround-sound system, and a stack of DVDs with my first big commission check. By nineteen I was making fifty thousand dollars a year, more than I ever saw my parents bring home, but I was spending sixty-five grand. So maybe money wasn't going to buy me happiness. Or maybe I just needed to adjust for inflation.

So I worked harder, seeking higher income, putting in more hours as my twenties evaporated. I celebrated my first big promotion at age twenty-two the same way I imagined anyone would: I built a house in the suburbs, financed with zero percent down. Everything in my culture reaffirmed this decision, even told me I was making a solid investment (this was five years before America's housing bubble burst). It wasn't just any old house, though; it was an oversized, two-story monstrosity, with three bedrooms, two livingrooms, and a full-size basement (the ping-pong table I hardly used came later, also financed). There was even a yard bordered by a white picket fence. I shit you not.

Soon after building the house, I married a wonderful woman. But I was so hyper-focused on my supposedly impressive career that I hardly remember the ceremony. I know it rained that day, and that my brown-eyed bride was beautiful. And I remember fleeing to Mexico for our (financed) honeymoon after the wedding. But I can't recall much else. I don't even remember the exact date of our nuptials. When we returned with sunburns and gold-banded fingers, I got back to work, filling our two-car garage with luxury cars and our new home with fancy furniture and appliances, stacking debt on top of debt in the process. I was in the fast lane, barreling toward the American Dream, a few years ahead of my contemporaries, who were all spending likewise, albeit five-or-so years later, rounding out their late twenties. But I was ahead of the curve—an exception, right?

After a series of promotions—store manager at twenty-two, regional manager at twenty-four, director at twenty-seven—I was a fast-track career man, a personage of sorts. If I worked really hard, and if everything happened exactly like it was supposed to, then I could be a vice president by thirty-two, a senior vice president by thirty-five or forty, and a C-level executive—CFO, COO, CEO—by forty-five or fifty, followed of course by the golden parachute. I'd have it made then! I'd just have to be miserable for a few more years, to drudge through the corporate politics and bureaucracy I knew so well. Just keep climbing and don't look down.

Misery, of course, encourages others to pull up a chair and stay a while. And so, five years ago, I convinced my best friend Ryan to join me on the ladder, even showed him the first rung. The ascent is exhilarating to rookies. They see limitless potential and endless possibilities, allured by the promise of bigger paychecks and sophisticated titles. What's not to like? He too climbed the ladder, maneuvering each step with lapidary precision, becoming one of the top salespeople—and later, top sales managers—in the entire company.[10]

And now here we are, submerged in fluorescent light, young and ostensibly successful. A few years ago, a mentor of mine, a successful businessman named Karl, said to me, "You shouldn't ask a man who earns twenty thousand dollars a year how to make a hundred thousand." Perhaps this apothegm holds true for discontented men and happiness, as well. All these guys I emulate —the men I most want to be like, the VPs and executives—aren't happy. In fact, they're miserable.

Don't get me wrong, they aren't bad people, but their careers have changed them, altered them physically and emotionally: they explode with anger over insignificant inconveniences; they are overweight and out of shape; they scowl with furrowed brows and complain constantly as if the world is conspiring against them, or they feign sham optimism which fools no one; they are on their second or third or fourth(!) marriages; and they almost all seem lonely. Utterly alone in a sea of yes-men and -women. Don't even get me started on their health issues.

I'm talking serious health issues: obesity, gout, cancer, heart attacks, high blood pressure, you name it. These guys are plagued with every ailment associated with stress and anxiety. Some even wear it as a morbid badge of honor, as if it's noble or courageous or something. A coworker, a good friend of mine on a similar trajectory, recently had his first heart attack—at age *thirty*.

But I am the exception, right?

Really? What makes me so different? Simply saying I'm different doesn't make me different. Everyone *says* they're different, says they'll do things differently, says things'll be different when I'm in charge, or I just need to sacrifice a few more weeks/months/years until I make it there. But then we get there, wherever *there* may be, and then what? We don't work less.[11] If anything, we work more. More hours, more demand, more responsibility. We are dogs thrashing in the collars of our own obligations. On call like doctors, fumbling through emails and texts and phone calls on the go, tethered to our technology. But unlike doctors, we're not saving anyone. Hell, we can't even save ourselves.

Someone yawns across the table, either Travis or Kent. Or was it Shawn? And now I'm yawning. It's not even 9 a.m. and I'm already on my third coffee, taking huge swigs, trying to compensate for last night's hurried, restless sleep. I'm tired of being this tired. I have nightmares about my job almost nightly. The nightmares often involve my boss yelling at me or asking me to do something I don't know how to do. I usually wake up panicked, nauseated with guilt.

The projector is producing the sedulous sounds necessary to keep its blurry image illuminated. HHHMMMMM. My phone, a corporate-issued BlackBerry, vibrates on the table in front of me. HHHMMMMM. My mother's name, "Mom," ignites the caller ID. I click the ignore button to extinguish the screen. I haven't spoken with Mom since…since when? Like, Thanksgiving? Has it been that long?

Mom moved to St. Petersburg, Florida, a few months ago to "retire," which I think means "to live off social security in a small, government-subsidized apartment building for seniors." I haven't visited yet, but Florida sounds like a nice place. At least it does in her emails, to which she usually attaches photographs of sandy beaches and of out-of-focus sunsets and, mostly, of her dog, a yappy Yorkshire Terrier named Sera (which is literally short for Serotonin), to whom Mom feeds ice cream and peanutbutter and parades around town in colorful sweaters with matching bows mounted to her little head. Sera is the center of Mom's empty-nest world. You can see it even in the pictures, mother and dog posed yearbook-style in their overstuffed apartment, cheeks and midsections expanding healthily, dolled up in post-retirement avoirdupois. They seem relaxed and happy and Mom appears to be sober, displaying her real smile through false teeth.

My BlackBerry's screen lights up again to notify me of Mom's voicemail. The meeting is adjourning: laptops close, overhead lights flicker on, a general sense of relief galvanizes the semi-sedate crowd. The room begins to evacuate, disassemble. All the smokers scatter first, jutting toward the exits on both sides of the room like they're escaping a burning building. It might be sort of nice to be a smoker right now, to have something to look forward to. I look up and Ryan is already gone, dematerializing as he often does. Moments later I notice his shoes under a bathroom stall's barrier, trousers bunched around his ankles, partially covering his four-hundred-dollar shoes. I'm wearing the same brand, black captoe Oxfords, polished and ready for duty. I'm washing my hands when I hear the toilet flush and the stall door swing open with great force.

"How are things with that new girl?" I ask Ryan's reflection in the mirror.

"Which one?" he says, feigning confusion.

"The redhead—the one from the bar," I say and pull a papertowel from the wall dispenser. Last week he introduced me to this new girl, who he seemed to really like, though I've forgotten her name.

"Well, how should I put this?" he says through a wry smile. "Her and I went out Friday night. Dinner and then drinks. Then we took her car back to her place. We started making out on her couch and you know, one thing led to another. We'd both had too much to drink. Things got a little weird. Not out of control. Just weird. You know, just tearing clothes off and stuff."

I fix my hair in the mirror as he continues this tale.

"Anyway, we both passed out at like three in the morning. But she had to be at work at like eight. So I slept in and told her I'd just walk to my car. Which wasn't that far away. Maybe like a mile or so. So no big deal, right? But the next morning, I couldn't find my underwear or my belt, and my jeans were ripped down the front at the zipper and her glitter was all over me."

"Glitter?"

"My walk of shame looked like I'd hooked-up with an undomesticated unicorn."

I look at him with half-scorn and half-envy. Although he was married at eighteen, Ryan has been divorced for five years, the same amount of time I've been married. I have it in my head that he is living the ideal life: having fun, doing interesting things, dating attractive women. I, on the other hand, am hardly having sex at all. My primary sexual relationship is with my left hand.

"What did you think about that episode of *CSI: Miami* last week?" Ryan asks, changing the subject, his hands under the running faucet.

"I didn't—"

"Yeah I couldn't believe it either," a burly Chad Ratcliff, director of Some Ambiguous Department, butts in. He sort of just surfaced out of nowhere; I honestly can't figure out where he comes from half the time. At age thirty, he's a dozen belt-buckle holes past his high-school prime, and accordingly he shouldn't be as nimble as he is when he weaves in and out of conversations. He continues maundering before I can respond, "That that guy with the Yankees hat was the guy who committed the murder earlier in the season. What a great, *great* ending! A great way to end the season. Never saw that coming, did you?"

"Like I was saying, I haven't seen the last episode yet. I DVR'd it for tonight," I say, soused with annoyance.

"Oh, my bad. Well, it wasn't *that* great anyway," Chad backpedals, pirouettes, and exits the restroom without grabbing a papertowel, his hands still dripping.

Ryan looks at me and shrugs.

The hallway leading to the elevator bank is mental-hospital white, steeped in vivid fluorescence, a windowless corridor inside this millionwindowed building. I'm frustrated. All I can think of as I walk toward the elevators is how much I was looking forward to watching *CSI: Miami* this evening, the highlight of my day. I imagine myself sprawled out on my couch, parked in front of my big-screen high-def television with the surround-sound going, sunk into the soft leather, laptop on my lap, responding to emails while David Caruso and his team of cops-cum-scientists solve crimes in the "steamy tropical surroundings and cultural crossroads of South Florida," just a few hours south of where my mother lives. It's not even nine thirty in the morning and a coworker has already managed to ruin my evening. I remove four Advil from my briefcase, wash them down with coffee.

The elevator dings, and when the doors open the tiny vessel regurgitates a handful of employees, leaving one other person in the elevator: our company's CEO, Rod Bracken. Rod is a man with whom you don't want to share an elevator. People, in fact, go way out of their ways, taking massive, often irrational, precautions to avoid the intimidating pseudo-interrogation that inevitably occurs during an elevator ride with Rod. I would personally run a half-marathon in stilettos to avoid being in the same claustrophobia-inducing space as him. But it's too late for me, and so I step on board and press the button for the sixteenth floor. *I can do this—it's just a few floors.*

"Heeeey! Jason! Good to see you!" Rod's false excitement interrupts my thoughts. I'm not sure why he thinks my name is Jason. He has likely mistaken me for Jason Epperson, a colleague of mine who has a somewhat similar role but who is also a foot shorter than me. Tallness-wise, Rod is situated somewhere between tall and very tall, roughly my height, and yet he seems to tower over me. He is expensively dressed, tailor-made everything; his posture bespeaks elitism. So far removed from my world, it's impossible to imagine him grocery shopping or folding laundry or jamming change into a parking meter. He speaks in a gruff smoker's voice, not unlike that of a conservative talk-show host. There's a hundred percent chance he voted for G. W. Bush—twice. But then again, I might have too; it's what you're supposed to do in this circle.

"How's it going out there in the stores, Jason?" he asks, a candidate's smile pasted on his weathered face.

Rod is savagely tan. He extends a large hand for me to shake. His grip is devastating. He knows I'm in charge of a slew of retail stores, but what he doesn't realize is that I'm also a director, which paradoxically means I don't actually spend that much time in the stores I'm in charge of, mainly because I'm here, downtown, wasting away in meeting after meeting: marketing meetings, product meetings, P&L meetings, operations meetings, merchandising meetings, customer-churn meetings, vendor meetings, customer-retention meetings, human-resource meetings. Sometimes we have pre-meeting meetings; that is, meetings about upcoming meetings. I wish I were kidding.

I consider explaining all this to Rod, but I refrain and instead reply with a delicate balance of vagueness and specificity, strategically crafted B.S. laced with a few data points that I hope will keep my particular brand of B.S. from sounding like, umm, complete B.S.

The elevator might as well be moving backward at this point. It's just now dinging for the twelfth floor. Rod looks at me solemnly. Can he see through my cellophane layer of gibberish? Then, quite unexpectedly, the moving coffer stops with a jolt, and I'm saved when the doors part like a scene from the Bible, and he exits onto the plush, wood-grained twelfth floor—the mystic executive floor. It's odd that the executive floor is on a lower floor than mine, as though one must traverse the depths of Hell to make it back to purgatory.

Rod looks back into the elevator, looks me in the eyes. "We need a good sales month out there. I'm counting on you, Jason," he says as the doors close between us. Relief washes over me. I squeegee my face with my right hand, breathing in through my nostrils, and after holding my breath for two more floors, I breathe out a deep, yogic breath.

The walk to my corner office—past cubicle farms the same color as Thousand Island dressing, past the piss-colored breakroom and its aggravating vending machines, past the cliche scene of two attractive young women talking at the water cooler—is unremarkable. A herd of smokers is returning, moving slowly around the foam-like dividers, more bovine than human, their teeth sepia in the sixteenth floor's emphatic lights. My corner office is less impressive than it sounds. The Lilliputian space, sterile and uninteresting, sort of looks like how old movies used to portray the future—faux futuristic, the future from the past. My entire life is inside these walls. Behind me, the view is of a high-rise building across the street, which is nearly identical to the high-rise building I'm sitting in right now, a view of their view of my view of their view, a sort of real-life M. C. Escher sketch. The rain raps soundlessly on the office's aquarium glass, thick and tinted, though you can't see the sky from which the rain is falling, just a jungle of vertiginous skyscrapers; without these tall buildings obstructing the view, you could see Northern Kentucky from here, directly across the Ohio River, four blocks south of my office.

I wake my computer from its slumber by jiggling the mouse vigorously. Phil Collins's percussion-heavy hit "In the Air Tonight," a song released the same year I was born, is seeping through my computer's tinny speakers, sating my Patrick Bateman–esque appetite for Collins's solo stuff. I can't help but sing along while scrolling my email queue: "Well I re-mem-BAH!" I even mimic the dramatic drum sequence that leads Collins into the final chorus: "Do-DAH-do-DAH-do-DAH-do-DAH-dah-dah." My inbox is bloated with two hundred and forty messages. We must be the only company in this hemisphere that still uses Lotus Notes. Make that two hundred and forty-one messages, still mounting. I reach for a paperclip and accidentally knock over my fourth coffee. The hot liquid seizes my keyboard and then drips from the desk onto my crotch. "Fuck!" I stop the runoff with half a ream of printer paper, each page soaked with my mistake.

My life occurs mostly in boxes. Each morning, I leave my box-home, drive my box-car to my box-building, ride the box-elevator to my box-office, stare at the glowing box on my desk, eat a boxed lunch, hop from box-room to box-room for various meetings (where we're encouraged to think outside, you guessed it, the *box*), drive my box-car back to my box-home, microwave a box-dinner, which I eat in front of the idiot box in my box-shaped livingroom.

I do this five or six days a week, fifty weeks a year. Lather, rinse, repeat.

Today at noon I eat lunch by myself, my only opportunity to satiate my unquenchable thirst for solace. The afternoon is peppered with back-to-back-to-back meetings—Meeting Monday, we like to call it—which I sit through with stained pants and a bloodshot heart. During each meeting, I nod congenially as people make their points; I interject forged enthusiasm at appropriate intervals, hoping to impress the people I'm supposed to impress. The meetings are over by five thirty, although most of my floor cleared out an hour earlier. But those pikers aren't on the same track as me. They aren't willing to sacrifice like I am to get where I'm going. Wherever that may be.

Sacrifice. What an interesting word. What does it mean? I often ask myself whether I'm sacrificing enough, but I wonder whether I should ask myself better questions, like, Am I loving enough? Am I caring enough? Am I contributing enough? I don't think I'd like the answers, so I dismiss the thought.

Each morning, I arrive at the office before sunrise, when the sky still has that predawn color of an overripe eggplant. Most days I'm the first or second person on the entire sixteenth floor (occasionally my boss's churlish boss is here before me, but I haven't seen him as much lately; he's going through a divorce that's rumored to be quite nasty). The trick is to get to the office early and leave late, effectively killing two birds with one stone: (1) the bosses are impressed by the sheer volume of hours worked, and (2) you get to beat rush-hour traffic, which is important since I live in a distant exurb (a suburb of a suburb), a commuter town parked halfway between Cincinnati and Dayton. Even when there's no traffic, it takes me forty-five minutes to drive home, three times that during rush hour. So I stick around the office most nights until seven, where it's just me and Omar, the friendly, ageless Nigerian cleaning guy who loves to overwater everyone's plants.

"Would you like me to empty your trash, Mr. Millburn?" Omar asks, just as he does every night.

"You can just call me Joshua," I remind him.

"Yes, sir, Mr. Joshua," he says and then removes the thin plastic liner from my waste basket. "Merry Christmas," he adds before he wheels and exits my office. He stops by each night to empty my trash and to say hi. We've established a rapport. I probably have a better relationship with Omar than with ninety percent of my family.

"Merry Christmas," I respond. I am seated in my office, catching up on the never-ending stack of emails and losing at solitaire. The winter sun has already set, a streak of blood-red twilight reflects off the windows across the street. I look down at my phone and remember to check my voicemail. "You have eight new messages," the robotic Anglo woman informs me. The second message is from Mom; her voice takes over the speaker. "Honey, it's me. Can you call me back? It's important," is all the message says, followed by several seconds of silence as she struggles to hang up.

Something's wrong. I can tell she's been crying. Her slurred cadence is outfitted in red wine, indicating a return to the bottle. Phil Collins, stuck on repeat, is still crooning through my speakers. I turn down the volume and dial Mom's number…but then pause, hovering over the SEND button, suspended in time. Moments go by staring at the phone's screen, waiting. I'm not ready to bear the weight of whatever she's about to reveal.

2 || Stray Age

October 2009

The atmosphere at Suncoast Hospice is so thick it's hard to breathe. The indoor lighting is soft and placid. My chair is next to Mom's bed, her small living quarters decorated with miscellanea, niceties strategically placed to make her feel at home: picture frames, artwork, and the like. A complex machine is set up next to us; it is large and clunky and has a pixelated LED screen meant to monitor her vitals. The machine is switched off.

Tears burn my cheeks. I'm crying for the first time in my adult life. A picture of Mom and me, the two of us smiling on a beach, is perched on the nightstand. She's wearing a smile and a blonde wig in the photo.

This morning I received a call to let me know that things had taken a turn. I better fly down, the nurse said. She tried to put Mom on the phone, but her speech was incoherent. She sounded unlike I've ever heard her, unlike I've ever heard anyone. Like a dying character from a bad movie, droning and gurgling, emitting vague sounds, not words. I told Mom I loved her and hung up the phone and then booked a flight from Dayton to Tampa and called Ryan to drive me to the airport.

I had spoken with Mom just yesterday. Her words then were slurred but semi-intelligible, and she was still conscious. Her short-term memory had been gone for at least a few months, ever since her cancer had metastasized beyond her lungs to her other vital organs and, eventually, to her brain, but her long-term memory seemed intact, everything still there, the good times and the bad, everything from our past frozen in time.

I sat in the passenger seat in Ryan's truck as he shuttled me wordlessly to Dayton International, my thoughts swirling under traveling Midwest skies. We were driving north on Terminal Drive, less than a mile from the airport, when I received the call. Mom was pronounced dead at 2:47 this afternoon, October 8, 2009. Ryan hugged me and I boarded my plane.

The cab ride from Tampa to St. Petersburg was navigated by a friendly black man in his mid-forties, close-cropped salt-and-pepper hair, a good friend's smile. His radio spat out back-to-back Michael Jackson tunes.

"You OK, man?" he asked, sensing my mood.

"My mother's dying." I couldn't speak about her in the past tense; I hadn't even seen her body yet.

"I'm sorry, brother," he said with condolence, turning up the radio to help me cope. "You Are Not Alone," played through the speakers, and MJ reassured me throughout the rest of the drive.

It is almost 7 p.m. now, last light draining from the Florida sky outside Mom's Suncoast window, sunset coming through the blinds in long repetitive slats. I've been here less than five minutes. Peace radiates from Mom's benevolent face, though it feels too cold to touch, not *cold* cold—not icy—but it lacks life, the temperature of an object, not a person. My sobs are uncontrollable. I don't even notice their arrival until they're already there, a natural reaction, like chemicals mixing to form an explosion, or tectonic plates shifting, an earth tremor of emotion.

She's tiny, lying there, fragile and small, as if her gigantic personality never extended to the size of her body. I want to hug her, to lift her frail, wilted body and hold her, to somehow bring her back to life, back to this world, and tell her I love her, tell her I'm sorry and that I didn't know what to do and that I wasn't the grown-up man I pretended to be, wasn't as strong as she assumed I was. I want to tell her that I would have done things differently. I want to yell this at her, at everyone. It seems we don't know how to love the ones we love until they disappear from our lives.

"I'm sorry," I say through the sobs. My shirt is wet. The room is inhabited by just me and what's left of my mother, her flesh but not her. She's not missing, she's just not here anymore. "I'm sorry. I'm sorry. I'm sorry," I repeat, rocking back and forth in my chair, a mental patient's sway. I can feel the wreckage on my features. The tears are a strange catharsis, a release of every spasm of guilt and rage and regret. But they are also a departure for me, these tears, a turning of a page I didn't know needed to be turned.

Eventually I have to leave; there's nothing left for me to say or do. I'm all out of tears, and so I hop a cab to Mom's building.

Her second-floor apartment is filled with at least three apartments' worth of stuff. So much stuff. It's not a hoarder's home, but there are a lot of material possessions, sixty-four years of accumulation. Everything, especially her hulking antique furniture wedged beneath dwarfish ceilings, seems too large for the space it occupies, like something out of a Tolkien novel. The livingroom is festooned with sentiment: dozens of framed photographs, overstuffed photo albums, artwork she has owned since I was a child. Ornamental embellishments have colonized every corner, nook, and alcove. Handmade white doilies cover most flat surfaces —more doilies than I can count.

Adjacent to the livingroom is Mom's kitchen, where cabinets are stuffed with several eras of mismatched plates and bowls and coffee cups. Every drawer is under the dominion of ill-assorted utensils. Inside the bathroom, a decade of makeup lives in a wicker basket next to the toilet, above which the shelves are neatly organized with enough hygiene products to start a small beauty-supply business. When I open the linen closet to assess its contents, I'm faced with stacks of mismatched bath towels and dish towels and beach towels, bed sheets and blankets and quilts. It looks like someone is running a hotel out of this tiny closet. I haven't even glanced at the bedroom yet.

Suddenly, it occurs to me for the first time: I have to figure out what to do with all this stuff. I sit on the couch and look around. Stand up again. Look around. Take it all in again and then close my eyes, breathe in through my nostrils. It smells like potpourri— fennel and rosemary. I walk over to her stereo, a hand-me-down from my teenage days. I have only one CD here, *Stray Age* by a Kentucky-born singer-songwriter named Daniel Martin Moore. I place it in the stereo and play the fifth track, "Who Knows Where the Time Goes." I've listened to this album every time I've visited Mom—seven trips, seven different weeks this year. Moore croons optimistically over a soft piano-and-acoustic-guitar instrumental, "Ah but you know, it's time for her to go."

It's dark through Mom's window. The lights of downtown St. Pete lead to the Bay, a sliver of which I can see from the livingroom. The water reflects the night sky, leaving everything bathed in a thousand hues of dark blue that stretch beyond the horizon. I sink into the ash-color couch, exhausted and unsure what to do next. I close my eyes.

When I finally peel open my eyelids hours later, I'm blinded by every bright surface. The morning sun angles through the windows, obnoxiously spotlighting my face and the objects in the room, casting shadows indiscriminately on everything that is beautiful and everything that is not. The white walls are screaming in the Florida sun. Everything appears bleached. I need a coffee and several ibuprofen.

According to the woman on the phone, they don't have a big enough U-Haul in stock. She says I'll have to wait until tomorrow. Which is fine; I have plenty of packing to do today, starting with the brimming bedroom closet. Why does she have so many winter coats? Doesn't she live in Florida! I mean *didn't*—didn't she live in Florida? I feel a pang of sadness. Surely she didn't wear any of these high heels. And pant suits? Really, Mom? Pant suits! When was the last time you wore a pant suit? And it's mind-boggling to see all these shirts and blouses with price tags still attached. Here are two bathrobes, unworn, "SALE!" tags still dangling like a friendly reminder of wasted money. Although I guess I can't point the finger, can I? I own a lot of clothes I don't wear, a lot of shit I don't use.

What am I going to do with all this stuff? I mean, I don't want to co-mingle Mom's stuff with *my* stuff, so that's out of the question. Keri and I already have our house thronged with our own personal effects: our livingroom furniture in the livingroom, our bedroom furniture in the bedroom(s), our entertainment-room furniture in our…well, you get the picture. I don't even have room in our vast basement, not with all the bins and boxes and assorted plastic storage containers from the Container Store.

Another phone conversation reveals that a storage locker in Ohio, one big enough to store (most of) Mom's possessions, is "only" [*sic*] a hundred twenty bucks a month. I'm not great at math, but my back-of-the-napkin arithmetic unveils an annual fee that approaches fifteen hundred dollars. Not exactly a bargain, but I guess you've got to do what you've got to do, right?

The contents under Mom's high-rise Queen Anne bed look like they were pulled from a bad mystery novel. There are several wicker baskets (picnic baskets?) filled with stained, off-white table linens (she didn't even own a diningroom table). Nearby, a boxed wedding dress takes up several cubic feet. Is it her dress? I hope not —my parents divorced in 1984, a thousand miles from here. And what are these? Three boxes oddly labeled 3, 4, and 1. They look like cases of old printer paper, kind of heavy. The cardboard is sealed with layers of brown tape. Here's a fourth box, numbered with a large numeral 2. Ah-hah! Rearranging the boxes uncloaks the climax of this Dan Brown–esque mystery: 1, 2, 3, 4.

But what is inside these boxes? The first box reveals the same contents as the second, which contains the same as the last two boxes: old elementary-school paperwork. *My* elementary-school paperwork, four years of it, grades (you guessed it) one through four, each box littered with English, math, science, and more English writings[12] (as it turns out, I wasn't that great at English, although my prepubescent handwriting is somehow better than my present-day hieroglyphics). Case closed.[13]

But here's the real mystery: Why? Why was Mom hanging on to decades-old schoolwork? She obviously wasn't getting any value from it. After all, the boxes were sealed, unaccessed for twenty years, just sitting there, tree bark in a box. If she were here, she'd probably tell me she was holding on to a piece of me in the boxes.

But how? I was never in these boxes. I didn't even know they existed until this moment. And yet she thought she could keep a piece of me—memories of me—by keeping these things. This thought infuriates me. Our memories are not in our things. Our memories are in us.

But wait a minute: Aren't I doing the same thing with her stuff? Except instead of little boxes under my bed, I'm going to squirrel away all her bits and pieces in a gigantic box with a padlock. And just like her, I will, in all likelihood, leave it there, sealed for a score in an edge-of-town storage locker, the final resting place for her belongings.

Faced with this realization, I pick up my phone and dial.

"Thank you for calling U-Haul, your moving and storage resource. My name is Randi. How may I help you?"

"Hi, I need to cancel a truck.[14]"

I was wearing a jacket when I left Ohio two weeks ago, but there's no need for one in Florida. It's still middle-of-summer hot here, scorching for mid-October: ninety-eight degrees, ninety-five percent relative humidity, air so thick that my hair parts in strange ways and frizzes like it's mad at me. I'm sweating just thinking about going outside.

I've spent the last twelve days divesting myself of Mom's property: her furniture, her clothes, even her supply of doilies, all of it sold and donated to help the charities that assisted her through nine months of chemo and radiation.

Into the heat of this morning comes peace, an ineffable weight lifted. I call a shuttle to drive me to the airport where Ryan will be waiting for me on the other side of my flight. I'm headed home with four boxes of photographs and many years of memories inside me. Before I exit the apartment, I turn around and take one last look at the empty space, staring into the vastness of everything that's gone.

The stereo is no longer there, but Daniel Martin Moore still plays in my head, "Ah but you know, it's time for him to go." Perhaps this is my Stray Age. Someone once told me that our bodies' cells regenerate every seven years, making us completely new people at seven-year intervals. I'm twenty-eight now. Maybe this is my fourth regeneration, my chance at a new start, an opportunity to be kinder to what I've been given, for that's all there is, and the meter is running.

3 || Blood on the Flag

November 2009

In the midst of all the seventy-hour work weeks, all the time spent on so-called achieving, I didn't *forget* what's important; I simply *don't know* what's important anymore. And so here I am, Sunday afternoon, counting the cracks in my wounds, sulking in my new bachelor pad, more confused than ever.

It's a dark apartment, stocked with brand new furniture and my own sullen disbelief. My mother's death still hangs in the air around me, and now, during the same month, my six-year marriage is ending. Shit. Looking around, it's hard to determine which way is up.

But even while Rome is burning, there's somehow time for shopping at IKEA. Social imperatives are a merciless bitch. Everyone is attempting to buy something that no one can sell.

See, when I moved out of the house earlier this week, trawling my many personal belongings in large bins and boxes and fifty-gallon garbage bags, my first inclination was, of course, to purchase the things I still "needed" for my new place. You know, the basics:

food, hygiene products, a shower curtain, towels, a bed, and umm…oh, I need a couch and a matching leather chair and a love seat and a lamp and a desk and desk chair and another lamp for over there, and oh yeah don't forget the sideboard that matches the desk and a dresser for the bedroom and oh I need a coffeetable and a couple end tables and a TV-stand for the TV I still need to buy, and don't these look nice, whadda you call 'em, throat pillows? Oh, *throw* pillows. Well that makes more sense. And now that I think about it I'm going to want my apartment to be "my style," you know: my own motif, so I need certain decoratives to spruce up the decor, but wait, what is *my* style exactly, and do these stainless-steel picture frames embody that particular style? Does this replica Matisse sketch accurately capture my edgy-but-professional motif? Exactly how "edgy" am I? What espresso maker defines me as a man? Does the fact that I'm even asking these questions mean I lack the dangling brass pendulum that'd make me a "man's man"? How many plates/cups/bowls/spoons should a man own? I guess I need a diningroom table too, right? And a rug for the entryway and bathroom rugs (bath mats?) and what about that one thing, that thing that's like a rug but longer? Yeah, a *runner*; I need one of those, and I'm also going to need…

Don't let Facebook fool you. There is one, and only one, accurate relationship status: It's Complicated. Such is the case for my six-year marriage. Whether someone has been married for decades, is recently single and dating, or is involved in some sort of abstruse polyamorous love triangle, all relationships—friendships, intimate, or otherwise—are inherently complicated. We are human beings, mixed bags of thoughts and emotions and actions, righteous liars and honest cheats, sinners and saints, walking contradictions, both the darkness and the light. The key, then, seems to be to work through complications before they mount, to find common ground and change course before it's too late. Although for some people—*ahem*—it's already way too late to course correct. We've all watched *Titanic*.

And so with all my apartment's new Swedish accoutrements, I forgot to buy curtains, and I can't find anything to cover the windows inside any of the boxes I brought with me. I wonder whether people on the street can see in? I can certainly see out. It's the first weekend in November, and autumn is falling down again; summer seems so far from reach. A few stubborn leaves still hang on, resisting their change in color, while I hang on to the past, resisting the inevitable. Most of the vibrant leaves, though, have already freed themselves from their oppressive branches. I envy their fortitude, their tenacity. They fall so gracefully.

My fall, however, is not marked by grace. No, my fall feels abrupt, steep, like the rocky face of a jutting cliff. But there is no branch that oppresses me. If anything, I am the branch. I have created my own totalitarian regime, one in which I am the dictator and also the oppressed people, a perfectly solipsistic tyranny.

My new furniture, pristine and showroom shiny, mocks me. A few framed photographs stare back at me with eerie yearbook smiles. They know I'm a fraud. I am seated on the leather couch, overwhelmed by what I should do next. Every possible action seems daunting, insurmountable. I let out a nervous laugh as if there's hope in this despair. Through the window, the afternoon sky is filled with opaque clouds that look like chalk dust smeared across the atmosphere, like something wrong was recently erased but hasn't yet been corrected.

Questions pile amongst the wreckage: How did this happen? When did our love grow cold? What was the first sign?

The truth is that Keri and I didn't have a bad marriage; we had a good one. In fact, that was sort of the problem: it was *good*, not great. More specifically, Keri was great—great in more ways than I can count—but I wasn't. I just sort of drifted through the relationship, my priorities far off course.

Sometimes we'd be out to dinner, grazing our expensive meals, and instead of discussing our days, our interests, our desires, I'd be on my side of the table, attending to the glowing BlackBerry in my hand, tapping away, responding to emails and texts, focused only on GTD[15] instead of on the moment and the real, living, breathing person on the other side of the table. After dinner, I'd usually return missed calls during the drive home, followed by hours tucked away in my home office, putting out purported "fires" at work, fires that existed mostly in my mind. I worked even on our honeymoon. I didn't listen, not really. And I certainly didn't contribute to help the relationship grow. To put it bluntly: I was kind of a shitty husband. That's not my special brand of self-deprecation; it's simply the cold truth. I never did anything egregious, but I hardly deserve a pat on the back for that.

During our six-year tenure, things spiraled without my knowing they were spiraling, and we grew in different directions. There were certain issues and concerns—important topics—we should have discussed years ago: children, short-term goals, long-term goals, interests, values, beliefs, desires. But we didn't. Well, *I* didn't. I avoided those topics like a boxer dodging jabs.

This couch isn't as comfortable as it looks. All the shiny new items adorning my new dwelling don't make it feel like home. Much like the rest of my life, this apartment looks good, but it feels empty.

I have to wonder: is this what my eighteen-year-old self would have wanted a decade after his emancipation? Sadly, yes, this is exactly what he yearned for: material possessions, a well-paying job, an expensive car, this lifestyle, ostensible success—comforted by conformity, not worried about the emotional price tag, nor the waves of hurt left in his wake. Look around. On the surface there's nothing wrong, but I'm not convinced.

The flames of consumption have licked at me from a young age. First, consumerism represented all the things I wanted but was too poor to afford as a kid: the video games, the logo'd clothes, the nice car. But when I began to acquire these things, my thirst was not quenched. Instead, the threshold for pleasure changed, the bar raised with each new purchase, each promotion, each bit of faux extravagance. Like a cocaine high, it is never enough; I always want more. I'm like Pavlov's dog salivating with adrenaline as the cash register dings its quiet celebration.

Now what? Did it take getting everything I ever wanted to realize that everything I ever wanted wasn't what I actually wanted at all? I'm encircled by stuff, all the things I was supposed to have, all the things that were going to make me happy, fulfilled, free. But I feel boxed in. There is chaos inside me. If it's lonely at the top, then it sure is crowded and miserable at the bottom. Whatever this feeling is, though, I think I need to feel it. I've been numb for so long, and I'm ready to feel something—even this, this wretched pang of loss and spilled sadness.

There's a large standing mirror on the other side of the room; it reflects a reverse image of everything I'm confined by, all this stuff. I can see myself in the mirror too, a lotus-eater. Is this what I've been waiting for my entire life? No. Obviously not, and for the first time in my life that's clear. I can finally see the pieces and how they might fit together, opaqueness washed away. I feel a twinge; I don't want *this* life. I want something different, my own deliberate life, not some nightmare that I've been sold as the American Dream.

There's nothing wrong with shopping at IKEA, just as there's nothing wrong with owning a couch or a television or any of this stuff. The items themselves are not the problem. The real problem is me. The real problem is that for the last decade—the last *three* decades—I haven't questioned my unchecked consumption. But our pacifiers can pacify us for only so long. Desire always begets more desire. And thus the American Dream is a misnomer, a broken shiny thing, like a new car without an engine. There is blood on the flag, our blood, and in today's world of achieving and earning and endlessly striving for more, the American Dream really just seems to imply that we are fat and in debt, discontented and empty, every man an island, leaving a void we attempt to fill with more stuff.

Lots of stuff. My unassembled bed frame is strewn across the bedroom floor in a thousand slatted pieces. Ryan agreed to come over today and help put it together so I can get the mattress off the floor. The assembly instructions don't have words printed on them, just a line drawing of a confused man attempting to put the pieces back together.

There's a knock at the door, six or seven rhythmic thumps. A glance through the peephole reveals Ryan in faded jeans, black teeshirt, and headphones. He's singing a song called "She Likes Girls" by a local musician named Griffin House. "I've got a girlfriend," Ryan belts out in an off-key baritone muffled by the door, "and she does too." He pauses when I open the door, and his blue eyes turn dark with worry when he sees me on the other side of the threshold. He removes his headphones and asks, "How are you holding up?" The question sounds still a bit singsongy but with genuine concern in his voice.

"Come on in," I say.

He steps in and looks around the apartment. The door shuts behind him. "When did you get all this new stuff?"

An iceberg moon presides over the denim sky outside my window. The stars are out, so bright they've rendered the streetlights redundant. My bed is assembled, and I'm alone again, memorizing the ceiling. Ryan is long gone. As he was leaving my apartment he asked whether I wanted to hang out this week.

"Maybe. Can I call you tomorrow?" I asked.

"Sure, if you'd like, but I'd prefer if you'd just call me Ryan," he said donning a goofy grin as he shut the door.

According to the clock dripping time onto the nightstand, it's 2 a.m. now. I'm just lying here, supine, beneath the stillness of my room, drowning in every word I never said. A scholar of the past. My eyes won't shut, pupils dilated under interior darkness and empty sheets. The cold caress of helplessness. Something has to change. Everything has to change.

Breathing into the room's stale air, I look at the window and feel threatened by the world beyond its panes. Eventually my eyes close without permission, the world lost inside myself. Throughout the night I take the dreams as they come, sorting through them one by one, each one more real and more intense than the previous. Most vivid is a dream of my drive home—back to the place that used to be my home—down empty back roads and snow-laden fields under drained Midwest clouds at twilight. The sky itself appears close to the earth, skull-colored, sprawled in stardust and angst. I'm driving faster than my instruments should allow. An unemployed scarecrow stands perched in one of the barren fields, waiting to do what he was meant to do with his life.

The car seems self-propelled, disassociated from my physical body. The arc lamps on the road are all switched off, forcing me to rely on my natural instincts and the vehicle's high beams to illuminate the journey. And when the headlights begin to flicker epileptically, and the blackening sky wins its battle against the day, I can't see where to turn or what to do, my instincts fail. The needle on the dash reads empty but the journey into the darkness doesn't stop, and then the car seems to buckle beneath me and the driving surface changes as I veer off the road, making it impossible to know which way was the right way and which way was not. I couldn't've planned for this. I clutch the steering wheel with both hands and jam the footbrake as hard as I can, waiting for God's wrath and hoping to make it to the other side with the least amount of damage possible. The sound of the cataclysm doesn't possess any of the shrieks or metal-on-metal tearing I expect, just the symphonic sounds of broken glass, the windows shattering in beautiful dissonance, disobeying the physical laws of the car crash, shattering before impact, breaking in preparation for the collision, not waiting for the accident but bracing for it. There is a cross of flowers on the roadside. And now everything is still, and in the darkness someone is opening the door for me. It's the out-of-work scarecrow. Outside the car there is a sternness of judgment in the barrens, shades of flamed earth under dimmed skies. One of the road's arc lamps flickers on, casting shadows on the bleached fields around us. Somehow the front of the car has wrapped itself around a telephone pole. The hood is mangled. A rise of smoke and the steam of half-a-dozen fluids plumes from the engine, reaching for the arc lamp and beyond, to the sky and the stars and whatever else was out there in the heavens spectating this event. My hands are bleeding and I can't form a clear picture of what has happened. It is cold. I wonder whether it's supposed to be this cold. The scarecrow is standing next to me, on the outskirts of the wreckage. In an dry monotone he says, "You were going in the wrong direction." It's impossible for me to disagree.

4 || Open Windows

DECEMBER 2009

My computer makes a funny noise every time it restarts. Something inside clicks and the fan whirls and then there's a beep as if something's resetting. December itself seems to be a reset month, a marker for when the current Now ends and the next Now is yet to emerge, hidden just around the bend, a time when the Old clashes with the New, unsteadily, abruptly, even violently, one unable to mix with the other, oil and water, concrete and glass, a Then that's not compatible with Now, Fear and Excitement swimming together at random.

The weatherman inside the TV on the other side of the room tells tales of an impending snowstorm. I keep the window open several inches, hoping to feel a chill, anything to let me know I'm alive. Everything is already blanketed in the world outside, big soft flakes fall and pile atop one another, a rainbow of white absolving everything of its sins. Next week will be one year since I received Mom's phone call, a year since things pivoted without my knowing they were pivoting, when time started changing and moving differently, more deliberately, time filling the spaces around me.

You can hear Ryan down the hall; he just left. We semi-successfully assembled my sideboard today with just one (large, gaping) scratch.[16] The sideboard is triumphantly situated behind me. My computer, recumbent atop my desk, projects its Windows Vista desktop wallpaper that appears indistinguishable from the vast fields you might see when driving west of Fargo. My computer screen is a sort of window from the banality of my world, emails and websites and now this terrifying thing called social media, all presenting different worldviews.

I signed up recently for Twitter on a whim.[17] Just moments ago, a friend of a friend of a friend—that is, a friend whom I don't really know at all—tweeted a brief message that caught my eye. The short communique is on the screen now, relegated to its hundred and forty characters of text: "How Colin Wright became a minimalist, said goodbye to his old life, and said hello to traveling the world," it says, followed by a link to a video.

I'm not sure why I feel compelled to click the link, but I do, and so I do. Click. Maybe it's because I have no idea what a *minimalist* is. Maybe I'm looking for any answer to latch on to. Maybe I'm just wasting my time.

After a moment of obligatory buffering, the video comes to life, opening with a logo for *Breakfast Television New Zealand*, a morning television show with comfy couches and bright lights, scrolling headlines and flashing titles taking up the screen at certain intervals. An orangish digital nameplate appears below the bust of an attractive twenty-something: "Colin Wright: Minimalist and Professional Traveler." The camera pans out to reveal Colin, a twenty-four-year-old Midwesterner, sporting a fitted teeshirt, a Kiwi suntan, baby-blue eyes, and a mane of untamed sandy-blond hair that crowds the screen,[18] sitting across from the show's suit-

and-tied host, late forties, outfitted in a Euro-cut suit. His co-host, a blonde woman—pretty, late twenties—blushes at the mere sight of the traveling American.

"You've been living in New Zealand for a few months now," the host says to Colin. "How has your experience been so far?"

"It's unfairly beautiful here. I feel like I could set my camera to a ten-second shutter release, throw it in the air, and whatever photo it takes would be award-winning." Colin has a calm, unrehearsed speaking voice, the kind that makes you listen attentively. He says that travel is his passion, but not just any kind of travel: full submersion into a culture, learning everything from scratch. Thereby, he moves to a new country every four months; once he gets comfortable, it's time to go, time to find somewhere new. The kicker, though, is that he doesn't get to pick the country. Instead, his readers vote on his next home country at his website, *Exile Lifestyle*, wherein every four months he tallies the votes, packs his carry-on bag, and hops a plane, knowing almost nothing about his new homeland—a sexy, made-for-the-movies lifestyle.[19]

I scratch my head—literally. I have no desire to travel the world as some sort of peripatetic writer. My idea of travel involves driving to Toledo, not Tanzania. Colin opines that something called *minimalism* allows him to pursue what he's passionate about, which takes me aback. What am I passionate about?

"Your website says you own fifty-one things," the host says, gasping at the thought. He adjusts his neck tie, which doesn't need adjusting.

I gasp a little too. Fifty things? I must own thousands—maybe tens of thousands—of things. Clothes, furniture, electronics, tools, kitchenware, decoratives, artwork, office supplies, the list stretches on. Plus all the stuff I have in storage—boxes and boxes of stuff— that I haven't yet integrated into my month-old living quarters.

Basically, I own a lot of stuff. Like, *a lot*, a lot.

After a pause, as though to emphasize the shock, the host continues: "There are photos of everything you own, right there online, correct?" The screen transitions to a photo of Colin sitting on the floor surrounded by all his worldly possessions, mostly clothes and basic hygiene products and a few portable electronics like a laptop and an MP3 player.

"Yes. I own roughly fifty things," Colin says. "But they are all things that bring immense value to my life."

"But *fifty* things?" the host repeats.

"Yes," Colin smiles. "But they're fifty really nice things."

"Doesn't that seem a little extreme—just fifty items?"

"The number itself is arbitrary, a factoid that people like to latch on to. The truth is that I own what I can carry with me when I travel—things that truly add value to my life."

"But then you have a storage locker back in the States with all your personal effects, right?"

"Actually, I don't have anything left in the US. I got rid of everything, even the paperwork—I had a Shredding Party."

"A Shredding Party?"

"Yes. I invited a handful of friends over, bought food and drinks, threw a Pomplamoose album on the stereo, and started shredding years of redundant and unneeded documents, scanning the ones I actually needed, all while 'Beat the Horse' ricocheted the walls of my townhouse. We had fun with it. A party."

"So you really got rid of everything?"

"That was the entire point. Part of being a minimalist is not just having very little with you; it's actually about *owning* very little. Because the act of ownership is what stressed me out, kept me from feeling free."

The *act* of ownership? Huh. I've never thought of ownership as an act. Although I realize that I too am stressed out by my belongings. And I guess it is an act in a way—the act of taking care of my things, fixing broken items, replacing stuff that needs to be replaced, and of course protecting my personal property so that no one takes it from me. A lot of work goes into simply acquiring and maintaining my myriad possessions. It weighs on me.

"It turns out that the old cliche is true," Colin continues. "Our possessions possess us. All the things I owned kept the back of my mind activated. I used to sit around and feel weighed down by all the stuff in my life. I'd worry about everything I had, thinking 'I've got this much, so now I need more—I need to level it out: I have the TV, so I need the DVD player; I have the garage, so I need a nice car to fill it; I have this, so I need that.' It's a never-ending cycle, a cold war with yourself."

A never-ending cycle? I've never thought of it this way. I've always been striving toward something, running toward some invisible finish line. What happens after that though? What happens when I accumulate all the stuff and make it past a particular finish line? Unsatisfied, I always immediately start looking for the next finish line.

The show's host, nearly catatonic with amazement, looks at Colin blankly. Finally he blinks, loosens his tie, unbuttons his top button. "What made you decide to become a minimalist?"

"I discovered that material possessions are nothing more than a blindfold, keeping our eyes from seeing the truth in the world around us. But I didn't always feel this way. Up until last year, I was living the ideal life—the so-called *Dream*. After college, I ran a design studio in Los Angeles, and I worked my butt off trying to grow my business, taking as much work as I could, often working a hundred or more hours a week. And I was wildly successful. I was making good money and had all the stuff to prove it. But all I was doing was working. I didn't have time for anything else."

The blonde co-host smiles bashfully for no apparent reason.

"The unfortunate thing was," Colin says, "my dream had always been to travel. But there had always been these supposedly more important things. Like running my company. Like climbing the social and economic ladders. Like my goal to make my first million dollars by twenty-five. Which seemed like a really great plan at the time; looking back, perhaps not so much. I figured you had to make a bunch of money *before* you could travel. In fact, until last year, my passport was empty."

"Interesting," the host says dryly.

"Yeah, well, it was the opposite of interesting. Until last year, I wanted to earn a million bucks—thought that would make me happy. I still had a couple years to go until I was twenty-five, and I felt like I could attain that goal if I stuck around and stayed the course. But whenever I looked forward a little bit, whenever I peered into my future, I could see what lay down that path. I'm not clairvoyant, but I had seen other people be very successful entrepreneurs, people who were doing similar things. They all shared one thing in common: they never leave. Once you make a million dollars, a million is no longer enough. So then you have to make five million. And then fifty. And eventually you've spent more than half your life simply trying to earn money. But for what?"

"What, indeed. Then how did you make the switch?" asks the host.[20] "Having this realization is one thing, making the change is another."

"I started planning right away. I wasn't entirely sure what I wanted to do instead of this goal that, for so long, had been a light on the horizon. But I knew I wanted to leave my options open, and I knew I wanted to travel. That's all I knew for sure. So I did what fifty thousand people do every day: I started a blog. I'd never run a blog before, but I'd heard it was the thing to do. For apparent reasons I named it *Exile Lifestyle* and decided it would be the online documentation of my journey, a single place to capture all the travel I soon planned on doing, and also the sort of online register to publicly record my change in lifestyle, from businessy man in LA to itinerant guy pursuing his dream of travel."

"Travel was your catalyst toward minimalism, then?"

"After I started the blog I started getting rid of everything. I knew that if I was going to be traveling, then owning a lot of stuff would be a hindrance. I could have gotten a storage space for it, but the overhead investment alone seemed a bit ridiculous—to store a bunch of stuff I, by definition, wasn't going to use—but also just worrying about all this stuff back home, all my things weighing down my mind. It turns out that minimalism would've been the right answer even if I wasn't traveling. It would've helped me free myself from the chains of consumerism."

"I see. How did you know where to travel when you finally took off?"

"I'd never left the country, and I didn't really know where to go. So I just asked the couple hundred people reading my blog. I let everyone vote on the country I should travel to, and the consensus was Argentina. The voting process went so well that I thought, Maybe I should keep letting people vote for my next country as I move around the world."

"And now you move to a new country every four months, and you still let your readers choose where you're going next?"

"That's correct. The readership has grown considerably, but the process is still the same."

"I think that's fantastic, but how do you earn enough money to live your lifestyle?"

"The surprising thing was that the blog helped me do what I was doing for a living—my design work—even better. I'd built a lot of connections in person, and I'd made a nice chunk of money that way, but when I started traveling and blogging, people who were reading my blog starting saying 'I'd like to hire you,' or 'My company would like to hire you,' and the quality of my clients now is even better than my clients in Los Angeles."

"That's astounding. Besides radically paring down your possessions so you can travel, has minimalism helped you in other ways?"

"Yes. A ton. Minimalism has allowed me to eliminate the other distractions from my life, things that, when you step back and look at the big picture, just don't matter as much as we think they do."

"For example?"

"Relationships that I clung to without a good reason. Bad habits. Silly activities that took my time and money and energy. Minimalism has helped me identify those things so I can remove them from my life and focus on things I'm passionate about, things I truly care about. Which means I'm able to learn constantly, which is really nice because I never feel stagnant; I never feel bored or like I'm not growing, because I'm *always* learning new things, always growing. Plus, because I've been able to get rid of so many material things, I don't get as attached to my possessions anymore, which means I can take more risks because I'm not spending money on a bunch of junk I don't need."

"You, young man, are wise beyond your years."

Colin smiles a thank you.

"Thank you for speaking with us today, Colin. Do you have any advice for people who are afraid to embark on something different from the status quo?"

"The first jump—that's the most difficult part. Because you'll always have some people who say things like, 'Why would you do that?' or 'How *can* you do that?' or 'If you could do that thing you want to do—write that novel or become an entrepreneur or travel the world or whatever—then everyone would be doing it.' It's important to remember that these naysayers are just projecting. It's that ingrained fear we all have, a natural instinct. We tend to be afraid of bucking the status quo. But when you do take that first jump, it actually becomes terrifying to do 'normal' things, because you realize what a risk it is to give up your entire life just to be *normal*."

The video stops. I look around once again at my *normal* apartment stocked with *normal* stuff. It's been over a month since I moved in, and there are still boxes I haven't unpacked. I've forgotten what's in the unlabeled ones, and yet they nag me daily. Every few days I unpack a box or two, attempting to move the unused objects from their cardboard containers to some other unit of storage: a cupboard, a junk drawer, a closet, a shelf, anywhere I won't have to deal with it. It's not unlike old-time prisoners forced to move stones from one side of the yard to the other, just to move them back again once all the stones have migrated. The stuff is always there, in perpetuity, moving from location to location, anchoring me, not in a good way.

So then perhaps jettisoning my belongings is the answer; perhaps minimalism is an answer for me. But I'm no jet-setter. I don't want to travel the world; I don't want to own only fifty things. Maybe Colin's lifestyle is best suited for, well, guys like Colin, guys younger than me, cool Gen-Yers who want to travel the world unencumbered by their things, not people like me who've climbed the corporate ladder, who've proven they can function in a status-quo world, we who enjoy owning a desk and a couch and a kitchen table and enough kitchenware to have a handful of friends over to share a homecooked meal.

I wonder whether there are other, different, less-extreme minimalists out there.

With a click, a new Internet-browser window opens to my search-engine homepage: Yahoo![21] The keywords "becoming a minimalist," "living with less," and "minimalism" yield results for three different websites: *Becoming Minimalist*, *Be More with Less*, and *Zen Habits*, respectively.

The aptly titled *Becoming Minimalist*, a website started last year by Joshua Becker, a thirty-four-year-old husband and father of two, who lives in suburban New England and works full-time for a nonprofit organization, tells a different story of minimalism. In an audio recording posted on his site, Becker tells the story of how he stumbled into minimalism.

"I think I have a pretty simple message," he says. "There is more joy and fulfillment in pursuing less than can be found in pursuing more."

This sounds like a platitude at first, but it doesn't sound trite. Becker's tone is calm and honest, his cadence genuine. "Unfortunately, since the moment we were born, we have been told the exact opposite. We have been told every day of our lives, through every advertisement—the three thousand ads we see every day on television, radio, magazines, billboards, and on the Internet—that we should pursue more, and that we'll be more happy, more *content*, once we achieve more. We've been told to work hard, to earn good money so we can buy bigger and nicer homes, so we can buy new cars and the cutest fashions and the most popular toys or the latest technology, and somehow when we begin accumulating all these things, our lives will be better. Life will somehow be more joyful. But we all know that isn't true. We all know that possessions do not equal happiness. It's just that we've been told this lie for so long that we start to believe it, our hearts start to buy into it, and it begins to affect the way we live our lives."

I think about my career and immediately realize this is true. I manage a slew of retail stores. It's my job to create demand. As Americans, our consumption has transformed from necessary to compulsory. It's hard for me to think of a single argument against this truth. But why doesn't anyone ever seem to break the cycle?

"I'd like to tell you a little about our story," Becker continues, "about how my family and I got to the point we're at today," It's clear now that he's speaking in front of a small audience, perhaps at a church. "They say that discontent is the greatest seed of change in our lives. My family, we had two streams of discontent that flowed through our lives like a polluted river. One I was very aware of, and the other I couldn't quite put my finger on until Memorial Day weekend 2008.

"The first stream of discontent was that I was never happy with our finances. Not that I wasn't earning enough money, but I was never content with the fact that we were always living paycheck to paycheck, always knowing that with just one lost job or one major housing expense or one medical emergency, our lives would be completely thrown into shambles. Plus I was never happy with the things I was spending my money on, never happy with where my money was going. I wasn't able to contribute to other people, to help the poor and unfortunate; I just didn't have the money to do that.

"The second stream of discontent, which I wasn't as keenly aware of, although I felt something wasn't right, was with the focus of my life's energy. All my energy was going toward the *stuff* that I owned, rather than toward the people in my life. I knew I wanted to invest more in my family and I wanted to be more involved with my friends and the people I knew, but instead I was always focused on the material things in my life."

I pause the recording. How many relationships had my pursuit of possessions ruined? And just as bad, how many potential relationships—new friends, neighbors, people in my community—had I missed out on while amassing my shiny treasures? It's impossible to know for sure, but I'm certain the number is high.

The audio starts up again. "My discontent, and a potential solution for that discontent, became vividly clear on Memorial Day 2008, a day that changed my family's life forever. Springtime of course means Spring Cleaning. My job was to tackle the heaps of stuff in our garage, while my wife, Kim, got started on the inside of the house. I don't know why, but I thought my six-year-old son, Salem, would enjoy helping me clean out the garage. I thought we'd have a little father-son bonding time together.

"That morning we woke up early and went out to the garage and began pulling everything out. I asked Salem to handle the toys. He got out a basketball and a soccer ball and, once he got his hands on the baseball and baseball bat, he was gone, off to the back yard, begging me to come play catch with him. 'No, no, I can't.' I said, 'I have to get this job done first.'

"This project of course took longer than I'd expected. After a few hours of organizing and cleaning and rearranging, I noticed our neighbor, Joan, engaged in a similar state of Spring-Cleaning paralysis. She happened to see that I was still working on the garage, that my son was in the back yard begging me to come push him on the swing. Peering at my overstuffed driveway, she looked at me and said sarcastically, 'The joys of home ownership.' I shrugged and sighed and said, "Well, you know what they say, the more stuff you own, the more your stuff owns you,' which is something I'd heard before, and I thought I knew what it meant, but it was just a typical canned response, one I hadn't really thought much about.

"My neighbor perked up a bit and said, 'Yeah, that's why my daughter is a *minimalist*. She keeps telling me I don't need all this stuff.' She threw a thumb over her shoulder, indicating her house and all its belongings. I glanced in the direction she was pointing and then looked back at all the stuff I was about to spend several hours organizing and thought, Hmmm, a *minimalist*? I don't know what that means, but I really like the sound of it right now."

(Yeah, me too.)

"Faced with a new awareness, I ran inside and found my wife cleaning the bathroom and told her about the conversation. She looked up and said, 'Minimalist? Uhh…I think I'm in. Why don't you go look it up?' That was all the permission I needed. I booted up the computer and did a search for minimalism."

(Well, this all sounds eerily familiar.)

"After getting past minimalist artwork and architecture, I found what seemed like an entirely new world that opened up in front of me—all these people all around the country, all around the world, who have made an intentional decision to live with only the things they needed. They were living with the absolute essentials for their lives, ridding themselves of everything else.

"Now, what I found is that everyone who embraces the simple-living lifestyle has his or her own flavor of minimalism. A minimalist lifestyle plays out differently if you're twenty and single, than if you're, say, a guy in the suburbs with a job and a wife and children. But even though this lifestyle manifested itself differently in these different people's lives, there was one common theme: they were all singing the praises of minimalism, talking about how freeing it was and how they felt less stress and how it made their lives so much better." Another contemplative pause. "That's when I made the decision to become a minimalist."

The next stop down my rabbit-hole adventure is *Be More with Less*, a website founded by Courtney Carver, a forty-year-old, happily married mother, living in Utah with her husband and teenage daughter. Like Becker, Courtney has her own unique story. In 2006 she was diagnosed with Multiple Sclerosis, a disease that has had a huge impact on her life. Even so, she doesn't let MS define who she is as a person. In fact, you wouldn't know she has MS if she didn't openly share on her site the lessons learned from her life-changing diagnosis.

Besides *Be More with Less*, Courtney runs *Project 333*, a minimalist fashion challenge that invites people to dress with thirty-three or fewer items for three months (hence the name). After digging deeper, reading more about various people's experiences with this project, I find it interesting, though not surprising, that literally thousands of people—women *and* men— have taken the *Project 333* challenge and have found immense benefit in slashing their wardrobe, reducing their closets down to the essentials.

Courtney posits a basic question on her *Project 333* homepage: "Does the idea of getting dressed in the morning with ease sound appealing?"

I look at my two closets, a large walk-in space and a typical wall closet, both chock-full of clothes: a dozen tailored Brooks Brothers suits, a half dozen pairs of Allen Edmonds shoes, seventy (yes, *seventy*: seven-zero) fitted Brooks Brothers dress shirts, five drawers full of undershirts and teeshirts, dozens of "casual" button-down shirts, two dozen pairs of jeans, eight pairs of khakis, three hats,[22] three pairs of gym shoes, a handful of "painting" shirts, eleven pairs of shorts, seven pairs of casual shoes, socks for days, unpacked boxes of who knows what. That's not even mentioning my coat closet, teeming with two or three (or maybe four) lightweight jackets, a wintertime puffer coat, a similar puffer vest, a heavy fur-lined parka, three topcoats, two trench coats, two leather jackets, three wool peacoats, a basket piled with scarves and gloves…

"You might think that editing your wardrobe sounds overwhelming," *Project 333* announces, "or that dressing with only thirty-three items is extreme. But the plain and simple truth is that it's not. It's easy and fun and freeing and, most of all, it's stylish."

When my immoderate wardrobe is all tucked away and hidden from the world, I'm typically proud of my Steve McQueen-esque sense of style. But now, as I stare into the cotton/wool/leather abyss beyond my closet doors, I'm sort of embarrassed by all the excess. McQueen wasn't stylish because he had two closets full to the gunwales; he was stylish because he was confident and simple. As Courtney's website says so eloquently, simple is the new black.[23]

The third place I visit is *Zen Habits*, which turns out to be a wildly popular website about finding simplicity in the daily chaos of our lives.[24] Created by Leo Babauta, a thirty-six-year-old man from Guam, currently living in San Francisco with his wife and six—yes, *six*—children, *Zen Habits* delivers easy-to-digest messages about clearing the clutter so people can focus on what's important, create something amazing, and find happiness. Leo's story is different from Colin's, certainly. But surprisingly, of the four intriguing sites into which I've dived headfirst, Leo's life most closely resembles mine (sans the adorable kids of course). Like me, Leo, who's also divorced (now remarried), used to be overweight, stressed out, unhealthy, uninspired, dispassionate, a cog in the corporate wheel. He worked a job he didn't love, lived a life that in many ways was not his own; discontentment seeped into the porous borders of his world. In short, he was unhappy. Just. Like. Me.

But today Leo is a simpler man, a man who has eschewed a life of requisite consumption in favor of pursuing his passion, which for Leo is writing.

Earlier, I asked myself a question: What am I passionate about? It's sad that I even have to ask, even more sad that I haven't given it more thought until now. Our culture, myself included, seems to be way too focused on "What do you do?," with very little, if any, emphasis on "What are you passionate about?," which in most cases those two questions yield radically different answers. They are incongruent. What I do to earn a paycheck—to which my easy, soundbiteish answer is "I'm a director at Broadspan"—isn't what I'm passionate about.

Unlike Colin, I'm not passionate about travel. Travel does not excite me. But, like Leo, I too am passionate about writing, albeit in a different way. Since age twenty-two, I've written pages and pages of literary fiction. I'm a fan of storytelling, of conveying the interior life and the human condition, of telling the truth through sensuous experience.

I am not, however, a natural writer. Hell, I'm more of a natural basketball player than I am a writer. I didn't read my first book until I was twenty-one. No lie: I was twenty-one years old when I cracked open my first book, Fitzgerald's *Great Gatsby*, and read it cover to cover. On the other hand, I was six-two in eighth grade, and thus basketball seemed pretty natural at the time. But as time went on, and I stopped getting taller, and my dribbling skills didn't improve, basketball became less and less natural.[25]

Years later, when I finally experienced what great writing could do, I knew I wanted to take part in its creation. By twenty-two, I knew I wanted to be a writer, because, as far as I can tell, good literature can produce a payoff unlike any other art form. When it's done well, literary texts are the only creations that impart an exchange of consciousness between author and audience, conveying raw emotion and internal feeling far better than Hollywood movies or trendy apps or even great music. It is this exchange that brought me to literature in the first place, when I was looking for something more from life than my long work weeks, an escape of sorts; and it is this exchange that still makes writing so thrilling for me now.

Unfortunately though, I wasn't gifted with a congenital writing quill. In fact, I was terrible when I started. I didn't know anything—not a damn thing—about grammar or syntax or sentence structure. I could hardly cobble together a coherent independent clause, let alone a sentence that felt urgent or interesting or even vaguely alive.

But then again, most things in life aren't innate. What I've learned from a decade in the corporate world is that individual betterment has little to do with inbred talent. Progress requires practice and dedication and, to a certain extent, a healthy obsession. Hence, passion is a mixture of love and obsession.

Unfortunately, "what I do" actually gets in the way of "what I'm passionate about," not allowing me to form the healthy obsession necessary to cultivate that passion. For the last seven years I've been an "aspiring writer," which really just means that I haven't written all that much, more aspiring than perspiring, as it were. Sure, I've *wanted* to write; I've even banged out a few stories I'm proud of (many more I'm not proud of), I started two novels that haven't gone anywhere, and even began a third novel late last year, the day I found out about Mom's cancer, a long thing called *As a Decade Fades*, filled with pages about coping with her death. Who knows whether that'll go anywhere. But while working endless hours—doing "what I do"—and watching my world crumble around me, I haven't focused on what I'm passionate about. I haven't made writing a *must*. Instead it's been a gigantic *should* in my life. I *should* write, I frequently remind myself. I should, I should, I should. I've said it more times than I can count —just shoulding all over myself.

It occurs to me that there are likely two reasons for this work/passion phenomenon, the epidemic of imbalance.

First, the question "What do you do?" is endemic in our culture. It is in many cases the first question we ask strangers. On the surface, it seems like an ordinary question, one we ask each other every day, a servile four-word nicety we utter so we have something—*anything!*—to talk about. Let's face it, though: the majority of the answers are boring, pungent ripostes we have standing by at the ready, prepped for the next dinner party or networking event or whatever: "I am a director of operations" or "I am a regional manager" or "I am the senior vice president of Who Gives a Shit." Whoop dee doo. Good for me, good for you.

Truth be told, we regurgitate these canned answers because they're easy to repeat, trance-like and semi-conscious, over and over and over again. I know I do it, rebroadcasting the same rerun, and I see it happening every day, everywhere around me. No one wants to talk about their boring day job ad nauseam, but it sure is easy to state your name, rank, and serial number; it's easy to prove that you're another cog in the wheel or a rung on the ladder—just like everyone else. It's much harder, however, to talk about other, more important aspects of life. So instead of searching for more meaningful discussions, we go about our days providing lifeless answers to this malefic question, our collective discs set on repeat.

But let's think about the question for a moment: What do you do? In reality, it's such a broad inquiry that *any* answer would suffice. What do I do? I do a lot of things: I drink water. I eat food. I write words sloppily onto little yellow legal pads. Once you scrape away its cheap gold-plating, however, we find a series of noxious inquisitions lurking beneath the surface. Sadly, what we're actually asking when we posit this question, albeit unknowingly, is: How do you earn a paycheck? How much money do you make? What is your socioeconomic status? And based on that status, where do I fall on the socioeconomic ladder compared to you? Am I a rung above you? Below you? How should I judge you? Are you even worth my time?

I've got to find a way to change my answer to this question.

The second part of this strange work/passion phenomenon is just as dangerous: for many years, I've confused *passion* with *excitement*. An issue people rarely talk about these days is what true passion actually feels like. Instead we assume that passion feels like excitement—that passion is inherently exciting—but that assumption is usually wrong. You see, it's easy to get briefly excited about something—an idea, a project, a potential promotion—and think that means we're passionate about it too. But this sensation of excitement about an idea is different from the type of deep passion that drives and fulfills people long term. Excitement comes and goes; it wanes when times get hard, when the work gets tough, when creative flow turns into drudgery. True passion, however, arises *after* you've put in the long hours necessary to become a skilled craftsman, a skillset you can then leverage to have an impact, to gain autonomy and respect, to shape and control your destiny.

Thus, passion isn't followed, it's cultivated. The thought that excitement somehow equals passion is simply not true, and believing the lie doesn't make it any truer. For any dimension of life, for any skillset—be it exercise, ballroom dancing, or writing—a person must be willing to drudge through the drudgery to find the joy on the other side.

People often avoid the truth for fear of destroying the illusions they've built. Up until now, I've done this only in the corporate world—when the reward was monetary—but not with something like writing, which better aligns with my interests, values, and beliefs. If I'm completely honest with myself, I haven't really spent enough time honing my desired craft; I haven't spent the time needed to become a craftsman, to be the writer I desire to be. Instead, I've aspired all over the place, writing haphazardly whenever I get excited—and I excite easily. I'll, time and again, get an idea that juts out of my skull and resonates with me so deeply that I'm impelled to put pen to paper and furiously create, to compose with vigor and excitement. But my enthusiasm always dissipates whenever I run up against the first hurdle, the first sign of tedium. Whenever the work grows difficult like this, I tend to bail.

But the tedium is inevitable. Writing is difficult. And writing *well* is, well, thorny and intricate and considerably more complex. It's hard, and who wants to do something hard when there are so many passive diversions with which I can fill my days? Besides, that smokescreen of passivity—anything that allows me to avoid strenuous work—is easy to embrace. It takes virtually no cerebration for me to flip on the boobtube and get lost in its blueish glow.

The aggravating paradox here is that there's nothing inherently wrong with ephemeral indulgences. TV and Internet and Facebook and everything else passive are fine in small doses. But there is no long-term reward for passive pliancy, just a beer gut and an empty existence, as I'm starting to learn while peering at my twenties in the reflection of the blueish rectangle glowing in my livingroom.

We all want to be something. Ergo, to become the writer I want to be, I'll have to find ways to make the menial work more fun, to do the work every day regardless of the result, to find beauty beneath the banality. Which means I must sometimes tolerate the pain if I want to pursue real pleasure. It'll take time and discipline and prioritization. Real prioritization, not lip-service. Writing might've been a *declared* priority throughout most of my twenties—after all, I really, really wanted to do it—but it wasn't ever a *real* priority. The reality of my daily grind is that life's mundane tasks eat up most of my time: Checking email. Monkeying around on the Internet. Watching television. Filling out reports. These activities are my true priorities.

I've always claimed that my priorities are grandly important activities like spending time with family or exercising or carving out enough alone time to write. But they're not. Until I actually put these pursuits first, until I make these undertakings part of my everyday routine, they are not my actual priorities.

This is going to change. Starting today. My priorities are what I do each day, the small tasks that move forward the second and minute hands on the clock. These circadian endeavors are my *musts*. Everything else is simply a *should*.

It seems that the current track on which I'm traveling isn't the right one. Perhaps like Colin and Courtney and Becker and Leo, minimalism would help me, not to deprive myself but to clear the clutter, to remove the excess and reorganize my life, to get on the right track. So far I've just waited for things to change, to mysteriously get better, waiting on some kind of luck to enter my atmosphere. But waiting without action feels wrong now. It seems like bad luck to simply put my faith in good luck. I know I might fail, but we all must fail from time to time—we have to figure out what doesn't work so we can find out what does.

I shut my laptop and peek at the window. It's dark now and all I can see is my reflection.

5 || Strong Moves Slow

June 2010

It had been quiet on the subway. What a nice surprise. Of course I don't comprehend the silence until now, after already exiting the J train. I'm approaching Times Square, swimming vigorously against the stream of people and the spill of electric light. Everything seems caffeinated.

I am here beneath the howl of the world, the pulse of a city dead inside, and yet all this noise is unable to wake the dead. Heads tilt downward, faces lost in glowing screens, technology turning people into zombies. The lights ripple in the high-noon heat, bending and flickering and dancing all around me, overwhelming and unforgiving, sucking the polluted oxygen from the air, spitting fluorescent fumes, a rainbow of glow that rivals the sun in the semi-cerebral sky overhead. I'm looking for Colin Wright.

It's a New York sunburn summer, a hundred and one degrees with humidity, the air waterlogged and dense. It's Saturday, a week before my twenty-ninth birthday. I've been here on business since

Wednesday, but four days seems like a week in this city.

My world is clearer as of late. The last six months have been spent simplifying, paring down. A slow process. But strong moves slowly. By now I've abandoned a shedload of material possessions, maybe eighty percent of my belongings, shedding the excess, the superfluous things, tossing a few items each day, donating to Goodwill and other charities and selling stuff on eBay.

I started small, asked myself: What if you removed one material possession—just one—from your life each day for a month? What would happen?

The result: I unloaded way more than thirty items in the first thirty days. Like way, way more. It became a kind of personal challenge, discovering what I could get rid of, what I could get out of my way, how many unneeded things I could remove from my life. I searched my rooms and closets, cabinets and hallways, car and office, rummaging around for items to part with, retaining only the things that add value to my life.

Pondering each artifact in my apartment, I'd ask simple questions like, *Does this thingy add value to my life?* I learned that once you gain momentum, once you feel the benefits of removing the clutter from your life, embracing minimalism gets easier by the day. The more you do it, the freer and happier and lighter you feel, the more you want to throw overboard. A few shirts leads to half a closet. A few DVDs leads to deep-sixing almost the entire library of discs. A few decorative items leads to junk drawers who shed their adjective. It's a beautiful cycle. The more action you take, the more you want to take action.

I didn't just "declutter" my life, though. No, no, no. As far as I can tell, decluttering alone is sort of a farce, a trend promulgated on daytime TV and trite magazine covers with stories like "67 Ways to Declutter a Messy Home." What we're not told is that decluttering by itself doesn't solve the problem, not long term anyway. Discussing how to get rid of our stuff answers only the *what* side of the equation, but not the *why*; the *action*, but not the *purpose*; the *how-to*, but not the significantly more important *why-to*. In other words, the *what* is relatively easy. We all know, instinctually, *how to* declutter—*how to* get "organized." But that's just one part of the larger issue. Instead of "get organized," I've decided I need to start thinking of *organizing* as a dirty word, a sneaky little profanity who keeps us from really simplifying our lives.

You see, our televisions would have us believe that there's a battle being fought on the consumption continuum, a battle between messy hoarders on one side and spruce organizers on the other. And from our couches it's hard to see who's winning. I'd like to posit, however, that these two sides are actually working together, colluding to achieve the same thing: the accumulation of more stuff. One side—the hoarders—does so overtly, leaving everything out in the open, making them easy targets to sneer at. Face it, we all laugh and point and say "I'm sure glad my house doesn't look like that," every time we see them on TV. But the other side—the sneaky organizers—are more covert, more systematic, when it comes to the accumulation of stuff. Ultimately, though, organizing is nothing more than well-planned hoarding.

Sure, both sides—the hoarders and the cunning organizers—go about their hoarding differently, but the end result is not appreciably different. Whether our homes are strewn with wall-to-wall junk or we have a color-coded and alphabetized methodology to camouflage our mess, we're still not dealing with the real problem. No matter how organized we are, we must continue to care for the stuff we organize, sorting and cleaning our meticulously structured belongings. When we get rid of the superabundance of stuff, however, we can focus on life's more important aspects. Said another way: I can now spend my day focusing on that which is truly important—health, relationships, writing—instead of re-reorganizing the basement. Once the excess stuff is out of the way, staying organized is much easier anyway; it's like getting organized without the stress of actual organizing.[26]

It took admitting this problem—confessing to myself that I was but a well-organized hoarder, good at hiding my shit, ostensibly tidy with my bins and storage spaces and a complex ordinal system that kept my hoarding tendencies masked from the rest of the world—before I took action and really started removing the surplus stuff from my life.

If the *what* (the *action*, the *how-to*) is easy, then, then perhaps we should be much more concerned with the *why*—the purpose behind decluttering, the *why-to*. It's true that the *why* is considerably more difficult to discuss, because unlike the *what*, which is fairly universal, the nature of the *why* is highly individual.

Ultimately the *purpose* (the *why*, the *why-to*) of embracing minimalism has to do with the benefits we each experience once we're on the other side of decluttering. Hence, removing the clutter is not the end result; it is merely the first step. Sure, you feel a weight lifted off your shoulders right away, but you don't experience lasting contentment by just getting rid of your stuff. Minimalism doesn't work like that. By simply embracing the *what* without the *why*, a person gets nowhere. It is possible to get rid of everything you own and still be utterly miserable, to come home to your empty house and sulk after removing all your pacifiers.

When I got rid of the majority of my possessions, I was forced to confront my darker side, compelled to ask questions I wasn't prepared for: Why did I give so much meaning to material possessions? What is truly important in life? Why am I discontented? Who is the person I want to become? How will I define my own success?

These are tough questions with difficult answers. But they've proven to be much more important than just trashing my excess possessions. If we don't answer them carefully, rigorously, then the closet we just decluttered'll be brimming with new purchases in the not-too-distant future.

So as my belongings went the way of the Dodo, and I started facing life's tougher questions, I felt less bloated, lighter, as if losing a kind of internal weight. I no longer needed the extra space in my newish downtown Dayton bachelor pad, so I moved from my two-bedroomer into a smaller (considerably less expensive) one-bedroom apartment, three blocks south. This new apartment has a view of the park across the street and is situated in a communal neighborhood in which people actually smile and wave and say hi to you when you walk by. Birds chirp in the mornings. My mailman and my nextdoor neighbor are both named John. It's that kind of place. This is the first time since childhood that I've known my neighbor's name, let alone the postal worker's.

It's weird: I guess you could say I'm a minimalist now. Although if you visited my home you probably wouldn't leap up and proclaim, "This guy's a minimalist!" No, you'd probably just say "He's tidy" and ask how I keep things so organized, and I'd simply grin and tell you that I don't own many things, but everything I own adds value to my life. Each of my belongings—my kitchenware, my furniture, my clothes, my car—functions as either a tool or brings some sort of positive aesthetic value to my life. That is, as a minimalist, every possession serves a purpose and/or brings me joy.

Over time, situations'll change. They always do. And so I'm forced to ask the same important question over and over and over again: *Does this widget add value to my life?* But it's not just material possessions at which I posit this question now. *Stuff* was just the start. I ask it too, in regard to relationships, Internet consumption, food, and any other potentially superfluous matters in life. I constantly ask because circumstances constantly change. Just because something adds value to my life today, that doesn't mean it'll necessarily add value to my life tomorrow. So I keep asking, and I adjust accordingly. I may never figure it all out, but I'm learning.

As the last six months progressed, I discovered more about myself than I set out to know, a consequence of taking the proverbial red pill. I learned about my consumption, why I'd been drawn to it for so long, and why it burned me in the end.

Understand, every moth is drawn to light, even when that light is a flame, hot and burning, flickering, the fire tantalizing the drab creature with its blueish-white illumination. But when the moth flies too close to the flame, we all know what happens: it gets burned, incinerated by the very thing that drew it near. For decades now, I have played the role of the moth, lured by the blue flame of consumerism, pop culture's beautiful conflagration, a firestorm of lust and greed and wanting, a haunting desire to consume that which cannot be consumed, to be fulfilled by that which can never be fulfilling. A vacant proposition, leaving me empty inside, further fueling the blaze of lust and greed and wanting. It's a vicious cycle. Accepting the flame for what it is, then, is important; it is necessary and beautiful and, most of all, dangerous. This is difficult to do, but it is how we wake up.[27]

I myself am wide awake now, emphatically awake, just a few blocks from Times Square, where the flame is red hot. I'm moving forward, present tense, attempting to leave the past in the past. My mother is dead; nothing will change that. My marriage is over; Keri deserves to be happy, even if that means she's happy with someone else, someone other than me.

Yes, I can keep my eyes on the open road now, ignoring the rubble behind me. With my life less weighty, I feel exhilarated—electric, like the digital billboards that besiege the cityscape surrounding me now. I can almost breathe in the light. Traffic skates past. Car horns attack my eardrums, muffling a million conversations transpiring on every sidewalk. This is the opposite of quiet, the antithesis of solitude and calm, beyond the edge of my endurance. It's crazy-making. The enmity of noise makes me yearn for silence's euphony, for a stillness so real I can hold it in my own two hands. But I'll have to wait. There's none of that here. I close my eyes and feel the urge to shout something, anything, but my vocal cords are merely a candle in the sun; they couldn't compete with this chaos. The god of confusion resides here.

I feel older than I used to, but in a good way: more mature, less impulsive, better adjusted. I catch a glimpse of my reflection in a storefront window and notice that I *look* older too. I'll turn twenty-nine next week, the hardest and most arduous and, in many ways, most surreal years of my life in the foreground of my rearview mirror. Looking forward, something else is on the horizon.

A few weeks ago, another Colin Wright tweet caught my eye. He said he was returning to the States for two months from whatever far-off, exotic country he'd been living in for the last four months and wanted to know whether anyone had a smartphone he could borrow while roadtripping the US with two women.[28]

Well, it just so happens that I'm in charge of a cluster of retail stores whose primary products are, ahem, wireless phones, so I responded to Colin's tweet and asked where I should send the phone—a gift for adding value to my life. He gave me a New York City mailing address. "I'll be in New York later this month," I responded. He agreed to meet for lunch.[29]

So here I am, wandering Manhattan in search of the Grey Dog, the cafe at which Colin said to meet. I have an old BlackBerry in my pocket, and I'm getting ready to give it to a guy I've never met—some 25-year-old guy from the Internet. It didn't seem weird online, but now it almost feels like I'm doing something shady, like a drug deal or selling illegally bred hairless cats on the blackmarket or something. It's a strange feeling. For no reason at all, I look over my shoulder in what I'm certain is a suspicious manner.

God it's hot today. Do I always sweat this much? I've been here only a few days, staying in Brooklyn, and I've already had enough of this place, every borough. If home is where the heart is, then my home is not in New York. Times Square is just the tipping point. I feel enveloped by this city, nowhere to turn for solace.

This morning I decided to see Times Square before I went to meet Colin. I've been to New York a handful of times, but never made it to Times Square. There's no real reason for anyone to visit Times Square other than the obligatory trip one's supposed to take whenever one visits the City.

To get to Times Square, I exited the J train at Grand Street and took everything in: Arenose-black train tracks below. Gum-stained concrete above. Subway-tile-lined walls throughout. An old Asian man playing Far-Eastern music on what looked like a banjo. A rat meandering through the tracks below. Two teenage girls laughing and pointing at the rat, pretending to be grossed out and shocked at the same time. From the subway station I ascended a perpetual flight of stairs, searching for some surface air, as a portly woman with a heavy Eastern European accent descended the stairs on the opposite side of a filthy divider rail. She stopped me and said, "I am not here," an esoteric declaration if there ever was one, a confusing paradox. Except it sounded more like "I am not here?" and she seemed to be asking where she was or whether she was going in the right direction. "Yes you are. You *are* here, honey," I said and touched her arm softly and keep walking up the stairs. I am in no position to give directions. I emerged from the subterranean congestion and heat and humidity to the New York City street-level congestion and heat and humidity. Here and now, a Saturday Babylon.

I'm out of breath, out of shape. The sun is the color of a water-soaked legal pad and is making my eyes water, even through these sunglasses. The ratio of beautiful women to not-beautiful women walking the Avenue of the Americas is staggeringly positive. Walking north I notice an inert homeless man holding a cardboard sign that says simply NEED MO PENNIES. A few blocks down, a rambunctious panhandler is sitting in a wheelchair smiling and laughing to himself. There is a sign propped on his lap: GIVE ME MONEY OR I WILL KICK YOU IN THE FACE. He has no legs.

I can feel beads of sweat begin to pool and trickle down the small of my back as I negotiate my way through the sea of bodies, a populous assembled by hurried movement, forceful crowds of Ray-Ban sunglasses and skinny jean shorts and deep-V-neck teeshirts and milk-colored earbuds jammed in ears and Chuck Taylor sneakers and colorful tattoo sleeves and gingham dress shirts tucked into crisp slim khakis and leather messenger bags and more cute summer dresses than I can count, a minefield of consumption, everyone striving to look different—to *be* different—but when everyone is trying so hard to be different, they all become the same, homogenized by uniqueness.

Everyone avoids eye contact, looking everywhere—*anywhere*—but at each other, a strange sort of social contract, controlled by mass confusion, bystanders willingly stranded on an island they don't want to be stranded on. Bodies move through streets and avenues in radial streams, displaced and separate, a continuous loop, alone in the most crowded place on the continent.

A businessman walks past speedily, rattling off a string of incoherent corporate cliches in rapid succession into his cellphone: "...yes, we'll need to *ramp up our distribution*...sounds like we're *locked and loaded* on this one...we can *circle back* and *touch base* in the *a.m.*....the *bottom line* is we had to *drop the hammer* on him... this is a *high-level initiative* from the *top down*...we'll be *bringing our A-game*...we just have to *keep our eye on the ball...et cetera, et cetera, et cetera*..." He actually said *et cetera* three times in a row, mid-rant, without stopping to take a breath. I keep walking north, realizing that in many ways I am just like him.

Up ahead, a Hispanic man accidentally drops a half-eaten mango while crossing the street and is almost careened by a tan Volvo stationwagon as it runs a yellow light. The volvo's bumpersticker says DEAR HIPSTERS, WE USED TO BE JUST LIKE YOU. SINCERELY, THE YUPPIES.[30]

A brother-and-sister duo chase a flock of pigeons half a block ahead. Just beyond them a blind man stands idly against a brick wall, holding a ragged paper cup and a sign that doesn't ask for money but says YOU ARE LOVED EVEN IF YOU DON'T REALIZE IT. His walking stick leans against the rust-colored bricks beside him. I can't help but think that the blind man might honestly be able to see better than me, better than most people congregating these crowded sidewalks, and so out of guilt I place a twenty-dollar bill inside the man's cup and then immediately regret it, second guessing my decision because I don't really know whether the man is truly blind or just faking it and I might need that twenty bucks later, and what if the man really is blind but plans to use the money for alcohol or heroin, which means I'm just adding to the problem, a willing accomplice to a victimless crime.

During my short walk to Times Square I am handed no fewer than half a dozen flyers with pictures of attractive girls, all standing half-naked in provocative poses, each possessed by lifeless facial expressions. With each leaflet dispensed, I feel a deep despair, a certain soul-level vacancy, a vast emptiness that's hard to describe.

So now here I am standing in the midst of the mayhem, Times Square. My pupils are dancing in the overwhelming luminescence, and I'm wondering why I even bothered to come here. Times Square itself is anticlimactic; it feels like it was set up to be this way, to leave a void you had to fill by buying stuff, stuff that is advertised on every flat surface in sight. It's the absolute epitome of opulence and consumerism and the hard-to-explain malefic side of capitalism. And it does an outstanding job doing what it was designed to do, to overwhelm people's senses with slick, cool, hip, new, trendy marketing. Standing here is like trying to drink from a fire hose: more than you'd ever need, and yet it could never satiate your thirst for more. It's painful if you're aware of what is going on, emotionally abortive if you're not.

The light inside the Grey Dog is filtered through opaque windows. The echo of the city is still humming inside me. Colin and I are seated at a four-top toward the back of the restaurant. I sit and listen, weary and thirsty. My shirt is sopping. Beads of sweat collect along the wrinkles on my forehead. My hair has been rearranged by the city's elements. This glass of ice water hardly soothes the absolute heat. The ice has already melted, and condensation rings form where the glass meets the table.

Colin is dressed in jeans and an untucked dress shirt that is as crisp as calloused hands clapping in winter air. He is somehow even more toothsome in person, suffused with confidence without a trace of arrogance. A mug is positioned in front of him; its steam climbs toward his face. He is seated upright, his posture speaks attentiveness. There's no A/C in this place, or if there is it isn't working, yet he's drinking something hot, defying all basic principles of human anatomy, not even a droplet of sweat anywhere on his person. His hair looks assembled, unaffected by circumstance.[31]

"Wayfarer," a song by Jay Nash, plays softly through speakers mounted to each corner of the cafe. Colin communicates in good intentions. He breezes through the highlight reel of the past year, an inadvertent smile on his face. "New Zealand was fairytale beautiful," he says. "But for all that beauty there's a trade off."

"A trade off?" I ask, still panting from the heat, my words a breathless stammer.

"Their Internet is horrific. They basically use Australia's backwash. I mean they're still advertising dial-up. No joke. Which for someone who makes a living online, it's a huge problem."

"Is this why you moved toward publishing?" I ask, knowing that Colin had written about pivoting his business from branding to publishing, which is one of the reasons I wanted to meet with him today. I've been writing fiction for a long time, and all I have to show for it is a stack of rejection letters from agents and publishers. So I figured: You know what, I've always been a DIY guy—I climbed the corporate ladder without the proper qualifications, without a college degree—and now here's this guy who is truly *doing it* himself, not waiting for permission to publish his work. I wanted to know how, wanted his insight, wanted to know what to do. Basically, I wanted to find a way in.

"It is," Colin responded. "For the first time in my life I found myself unable to fulfill my clients' needs. So I had to slowly whittle away my little black book of clients, hand them off to people who could better service their needs. It was hard. I sat there and thought, What the hell do I do now?"

"Ouch. A dash of cold water."

"It was. But it was also good that this happened. Because not having that constant connection to everything and everyone gives you a lot of time to think. And what I realized from running a blog was that publishing content didn't require me to have constant access to clients. As long as I had a periodic connection, I could publish my writing online on *my* schedule, not someone else's. That's when I realized I should refocus my efforts from client work to publishing my own work."

"Publishing in what sense?"

"Well, up to that point the only real publishing experience I had was my blog. I did some journalism and poetry stuff back in college, but that was different from what I was looking to do going forward—publishing on my own."

"Like vanity publishing? Or like self-publishing?"

"*Independent* publishing," he corrects me. His subtle distinction suggests a vast delta between our definitions.

"What's the difference?"

"When I think about self-publishing, I think of poor quality, weak writing, someone who's not good enough to get picked by the Big Six. But when I think of independent publishing, I think *indie*. And when I think *indie*, I think artisanal and cool and raw and subversive—like indie music or indie films. I guess you could say that self-publishing is to indie publishing, what garage bands are to indie bands, or home movies are to indie films."

"Sounds like the biggest difference is quality."

"Yes, for the most part. Also, distribution. Which meant I needed to build a larger audience—a dedicated tribe of people who would support my work. I knew that was important. And because I wanted to *own* my own work, I knew I'd have to build that audience on my own. So I wrote two books and gave them away for free as ebooks. The only catch? I asked people to share those books with other people if they enjoyed them. Turns out they did. A lot. Both books have more than a hundred thousand downloads in a few short months."

"Wow. I bet that takes a lot of back-end work, a ton of self-promotion."

"It required a fair amount of work, yes. Wasn't easy."

"Sounds daunting."

"It's exciting. Think about it: I have control of everything—my audience, my work, my own destiny. Now that I have an audience, they are willing to support my future work. Not just willing, but *eager* to support my work because they find value in it. It's a lot of work, but it's freeing. I'm in control of the whole process."

"No more worshiping at the altar of the old guard."

"Exactly. Say, do you have experience with such worship?"

"I've been writing fiction for the best part of a decade."

"Ever had anything published?"

"Nope, not really," I say. "Scads of rejection letters, though."

"Are you any good?" he asks in not an unkind way.

"Yes," I hear myself acknowledge for the first time aloud.

"Really?"

"Without question," I say, knowing that during the past six months I've improved exponentially, writing daily, becoming obsessed with the craft. I've taken something I was good at and started working my way toward greatness.

"How good?"

"Empty pages aren't safe in my presence."

Colin chortles and then gestures toward the brown paper napkin on the table in front of me, "Hell, napkins aren't even safe around you."

I smile. The napkin is filled with red ink, front and back.

"How often do you write?" he asks.

"I wake up at 4:45 every morning, an hour before I have to get ready for work, and I write for at least an hour, sometimes much longer. I give up sleep to write if I have to."

"You should start a blog."

One thought enters my mind: What the hell is a blog? I mean I've heard him use the word, but I'm not entirely sure what it means. "A blog?" I say.

"Yes. You should seriously consider it. If you're good, and it sounds like you are, there's no better way to gain an audience. If people find value in your writing, it will spread over time."

I nod politely but pretty much dismiss the whole idea the moment it exits his mouth. I honestly don't know what a blog even is, even after reading Colin's and Becker's and Courtney's and Leo's blogs, which I thought were just called "websites," not "blogs." To me, a *blog* sounds like some sort of recondite Internet-thing on which eighty-three-year-old grandmothers catalog pictures of their cats.[32] Plus, what do I know about starting a blog? I can hardly spell HTML, let alone construct something that'd look good or resonate with people. I learned to type on a typewriter for Pete's sake. Email was foreign to me until 2002, at age twenty-one, when Broadspan finally forced all employees to use it, which I did begrudgingly. Nope, a blog, whatever that is, is out of the question.

"Thanks. I'll think about it," I say.

"Let me know how it goes."

"OK.… Oh, I almost forgot. Your new phone." I extract the BlackBerry from my pocket and set it on the table. Three twenty-something girls, each solo at her own table, simultaneously stare in our direction; from their googly eyes I can tell they're clearly not looking at me.

Ryan's shiny blue pickup is waiting outside the airport, double-parked next to a NO PARKING sign,[33] hazard lights marking my return to Ohio. It's hot, but at least there's air conditioning. The truck's cabin is littered with odds and ends. Equipment and gadgets and paperwork, clothes and tools and various appurtenances. There's barely room for my duffle. The sun hangs high overhead, a peephole view of our ride.

"I've been meaning to ask you something," Ryan says from behind the wheel. We're driving I-75 southbound toward downtown Dayton.

"Shoot."

"Umm, well…I'm not really sure how to say this."

"Say what?"

"Why the hell are you so happy lately?"

"What?"

"Well it's just that I've noticed a huge difference in your demeanor the past few months. You're like, umm, you're happy."

"Yeah, so?"

"You used to be this big ball of stress. Like all the time. But now you're so damn calm, and you seem content. You look thinner too, healthier. What's been going on? Everything alright? You're not suicidal are you?"

I chuckle. Then I explain the last eight months. How I embraced minimalism and how it has helped me focus on my priorities. How I started jettisoning most of my material possessions. How I'm living more healthily, writing more fiction, and paying off Herculean amounts of debt. How I'm even learning to play guitar, something I've wanted to do for years. I realize that I haven't shared this journey with anyone yet. For fear of judgment, perhaps, or fear of failure. But I haven't failed, I'm succeeding. I'm happier than I've been in a long time. And now for the first time since simplifying, someone is noticing the benefits I'm experiencing.

"Minimalism, eh?" Ryan asks after my long monologue.

"I think it might work for you too."

"You think?"

I raise my arms to illustrate the truck's cluttered cabin.

"What? This?" Ryan asks rhetorically. "I'm just a little late on my spring cleaning, that's all."

"It's almost July."

"So?"

"So you've got a lot of shit.[34]"

6 || The Sound of Minimalism

NOVEMBER 2010

This party is the least lame party I've attended in a while. There's great music (I picked it). The atmosphere is pretty chill (we're at Ryan's condo). Plus there're cool people here (it's just Ryan and me right now). And soon there'll be food delivered by the Chinese restaurant down the street. I hope the folks from China Garden find the address. When Ryan placed our order, the man on the phone asked him for his "street name" in broken English. "They call me El Greco," was Ryan's gruff response.

It's no secret among my friends that I am no fan of parties. Any event with "Fun!" as a requirement seems rather suspect to me. This party is different, though. This is sort of Ryan's minimalism-test-drive event. But because he's less patient than I am,[35] we've devised a plan to help him embrace minimalism more expediently than my slow, eight-month paring-down process.

So we decided to have a Packing Party.[36] Today we are spending the entire day packing everything in Ryan's two thousand square-foot condo.

"Pass me that Sharpie," Ryan says from around the corner. I peek my head past the obstructing wall. Ryan is wearing a green teeshirt that shows a camel's silhouette above text that says WANNA HUMP? Empty boxes occupy most of his *second* livingroom. Why he needs two livingrooms in his three-bedroom condo, I'll never know.[37]

Ryan just finished removing the last pieces of generic artwork from the walls. Save for the screw and nail holes at various heights,[38] the room is now stark.

Our plan: box up all of Ryan's belongings as if he is moving.[39] Absolutely everything. His clothes, dishes, and electronics. His towels, cleaning supplies, and toiletries. Even his furniture, most of which is too big to "pack," so we're covering everything with sheets, concealing his couches and tables and multiple TVs, making those larger items inaccessible until he "unpacks" them. Once it's all stowed away in carefully labeled cardboard containers, Ryan is going to unpack items only as he needs them for the next twenty-one days. At the end of three weeks he plans to do one of three things with everything remaining in boxes: sell, donate, trash.

I'm currently standing in the kitchen, eyes wide as a suburban kid's on Christmas morning, a giant trashbag in my left hand, while my right is doing all the work. Ryan gave me permission to throw out "a few things"—whatever items I think won't be missed. Holding open the mouth of the fifty-gallon bag, I'm sweeping in as much as I can before he catches on.

"Hey! What are you doing?" Ryan shouts from the adjacent livingroom—livingroom number one—where he just covered the coffeetable with a Teletubbies bedsheet. I have no idea how/why he owns that sheet.[40]

"Nothing," I say. "Just getting rid of some trash." I've come to realize that it's so much easier to dispose of other people's shit. The personal attachment isn't there. This is especially true after embracing minimalism myself. It's just stuff. Junk. Trash.

"Whoa, whoa, whoa," he storms into the room. His bare feet make a funny combination of suction and sliding sounds on the tile floor. "Don't pitch this," he says, reaching into the half-full trashbag, pulling out a mucus-colored mug with WORLD'S #1 GRANDDAD typeset across the side in Comic Sans.

"Really? I didn't know you were a grandfather."

"Yeah well I might need it. And these, don't throw out these extra cables."

"Extra cables? What are they for?"

"I don't know, but I might need them someday. Let's hold on to them."

"Why?"

"Just in case."

Ah, those three delicate words: just in case. I know them too well. For the longest time I had an intimate relationship with *just in case*. I held on to hundreds—maybe thousands—of things, *just in case* I needed them. Too often I didn't let go because I *might* need some miscellaneous material possession in some distant hypothetical future. Even when I'd travel, I'd always pack way too much—*just in case*.

But this year, as I began repudiating myself of excess stuff, I realized I needn't hold on to my just-in-case items. The truth is that I rarely use my just-in-case things, and thus they pretty much just sit there, take up space, get in the way, and weigh me down big time. Most of the time they aren't items I'll ever need.

Accordingly, I developed a theory a few months ago. I call it the 20/20 Theory: basically, anything I jettison can be replaced for less than twenty dollars, in less than twenty minutes from my current location—*if* I discover I truly need to replace it.

This theory has held true one hundred percent of the time so far. Although I've rarely had to replace a just-in-case item, I've never had to pay more than twenty bucks or drive farther than twenty minutes out of my way to replace it. (N.B. the three just-in-case items I've replaced are: a pair of scissors, a pair of gym shorts, and a modern-American-usage dictionary.)

My guess is that my little theory works like ninety-nine percent of the time for like ninety-nine percent of all items (and ninety-nine percent of all people).[41] What I've found is that when I remove the just-in-case items from my life, I free up the space they consume—the physical and mental spaces they occupy. More importantly, I haven't missed any of the hundreds of items I've gotten rid of—the stacks of magazines, the extra kitchenware, the clothes I hadn't worn in months, the extra coats, the extra shoes, and all the extra junk that cluttered my life *just in case* I needed it. Turns out I didn't really *need* any of it. Now anytime I feel the urge to hold on to something, I get rid of it as soon as I hear myself think those three words: just in case.

Ryan is standing in front of me, his GRANDDAD mug clinched in his left fist, a wad of electrical cables balled up in his right. The cables look like a clump of black seaweed. There seems to be a little fear, or an intense anxicty, in his expression.

"Let's just box up the stuff unless you're a hundred percent sure it's trash," he says.

"Are you sure this stuff isn't just trash?" I ask.

"Look, if I tell you a joke, will you promise to not throw out any of my stuff?"

"Maybe," I say. Ryan's jokes are usually great, though often for the wrong reasons.

"Why did the chicken cross the road?"

"I don't know, but I'm tired of living in a world in which we always question the chicken's motives."

"Just please help me box this stuff up," he pleads.

"Alright."

Nine hours and two China Garden deliveries later, everything is packed. My portable stereo is still going. Coldplay's Chris Martin is crooning the second verse to "Square One," while we sit on the floor in livingroom number two. Everything Ryan owns—every single thing he's worked for over the past decade—is here in this room. Boxes are stacked atop each other, more than halfway to the twelve-foot ceiling in some cases. My hands smell like cardboard. Every totem in each boxed tower is labeled so Ryan knows where to go when he needs a particular item: LIVINGROOM #1, KITCHEN—DISHES, LIVINGROOM #2, BEDDING, KITCHEN—UTENSILS, BATHROOM #2, JUNK DRAWER #1, BEDROOM CLOSET #4—PANTS, BOOKS #4, GUEST BEDROOM, JUNK DRAWER #7, and so on.

We're both tired, out of breath. I'm sitting atop BOOKS #6. "I didn't realize you owned this many books," I say.

"Me neither. Didn't you used to have a ton of books too?"

"I did."

"More than this?"

"Yes. A whole hoard of books. Like maybe two thousand. Maybe more."

"Two thousand. Wow. Were they mostly what? Fiction? Business books?"

"Man I had all kinds of books: hardcovers, paperbacks, trade paperbacks, literary fiction, writing and grammar books, photography books, self-help books, coffeetable books, old medical journals, genre fiction—"

"Those cute little pop-up books? I bet you had some of those," he says, unfolding his hands as if something will jut up from the folds.

"You name it. Shelves and shelves and more shelves, all nearly toppling with books," I pause. "Some of which I'd actually read, and many of which I planned on reading—someday. You know, whenever I got around to it."

"I know what you mean. But you never get around to it."

"Yeah, I know. Who was I kidding?"

"Why'd you have so many books, then?"

"To be honest, I thought my overflowing bookshelves made me look important and intelligent and cool. Like, *look at me, I know how to read—a lot!*"

"An *impressive* collection."

"What's worse, I thought my books made me somebody—someone important. Ironically though, it was a few quotes from a particular book I owned—Chuck Palahniuk's *Fight Club*—that inspired me to start getting rid of some of my books."

"Which quotes?"

"There were two of them that really stood out, and I'm paraphrasing here: Palahniuk wrote something like, 'Reject the basic assumptions of civilization, especially the importance of material possessions,' and 'The things you own end up owning you.' Both quotes kind of woke me up, made me look at the things I was collecting differently, which led me to another powerful line from that same book: 'It's only after we've lost everything that we're free to do anything.'"

"That's a great line."

"I agree. Those words resonated with me deeply. Like I could *feel* what he was saying—feel it on my nerve-endings. Within a week I sold or donated like ninety percent of my books and purchased a Kindle, which is where I tend to get new books now."

"What if you want a book that's not available electronically yet?"

"I don't run into that problem that often, but when I do I can get those books elsewhere—a public library, an indie bookstore, online. When I'm done reading it, I usually donate it. It's kind of funny: I no longer own piles of books, but I read more than before."

Ryan is nodding his head.

"It's kind of sad how much value I was placing in the heaps of books I owned. Obviously it was more than their real value. The real value was in the words—in the act of reading—not in the physical books themselves. There's no value in having a room full of books you don't need—especially when other people can get value from those books."

"So which books did you keep, then?"

"I kept only my favorite physical books, and what I ended up with was a carefully curated bookcase with all the books that add the most value to my life—books that I still reference from time to time."

"Was it hard to let go of the others?"

"Yes. Because I realized that they were a part of my identity. A part of me. And once something's a part of your identity—once it becomes a part of you—it's hard to shed."

"Incredibly hard," Ryan says. "I guess that's true for anything we allow to become part of our identities, though. Like our careers, our cars, our homes, our possessions, our sentimental items, our silly DVD collections," he points at two large boxes labeled DVDS #1 and DVDS #2. He hangs his head in artificial shame.

"As a former *collector*, I agree," I say. "I'll even take it a step further: I think the *act of collecting* is dangerous."

"Dangerous?"

"Yes. It can be. Collecting material possessions is, in many ways, not unlike hoarding. The word *collector* just sounds prettier than its alternative."

"What are you talking about? Collecting isn't the same thing as hoarding. It's like the exact opposite."

"Not really. Most of the time, yes, it is exactly like hoarding."

Ryan looks at me suspiciously, as if I've broken wind in front of him.

"Don't believe me? Let's look it up." I queue up the thesaurus app on my phone, which lists the following synonyms under the first definition of collection: pile, heap, stockpile, *hoard*. I hand the phone to Ryan with a raised eyebrow.

He reads it and shakes his head with acceptance and hands back my phone.

"It's strange," I say, "there're myriad TV shows and websites and clubs all dedicated to collecting things—not *creating* things, but collecting them. And while I don't think there's anything inherently wrong with owning material possessions, I do wonder why so many of us collect things? What's the purpose? Why do we give our belongings so much meaning? If we truly get value from the collection, then great—I say collect away. But often these things we collect add no value to our lives, and instead become part of us, malevolent anchors."

"*Anchors?*"

"Yes. Anchors."

"That's interesting. I've never thought of an anchor as a bad thing. I tend to say that well-adjusted people—you know, successful people—are *anchored.*

"Right. I've heard a lot of people call me *anchored*—as a compliment."

"That's true. We use it as a compliment without really thinking about it."

"But I like to take these sort of commonly accepted truisms and flip them on their axes."

"To explore the other side of platitudes."

"Exactly. *Anchored* might mean *well-adjusted* to some people, but think about it—what is an anchor? Like in the real-life, physical sense."

"The thing that keeps a ship at bay."

"Yes. Planted in the harbor. Stuck in one place. Unable to explore the freedom of the sea."

"Shit. You're right."

"As a couple of anchored guys, we both have a lot of anchors, right? Like, we have a lot of things that keep us from being free—stuff that keeps us from being happy," I open my arms, indicating the room around us, filled with material possessions. "Perhaps being *anchored* isn't necessarily a good thing."

"You've obviously thought about this a lot lately."

"I have. When my mom discovered her cancer like two years ago, I sat down and catalogued all my personal anchors, all the circumstances that keep me from realizing real freedom. It was eye-opening."

"Eye-opening, how?"

"My anchors were plentiful. I filled three notebook pages—eighty-three anchors in total."

"Eighty-three?" Ryan asks, incredulously.

"Eighty. Three. It turned out that being an anchored person was a terrible thing."

"Your anchors kept you from leading the life you wanted to lead?"

"Yes, and some of them still do. I don't think all anchors are bad, but the majority of them prevent us from encountering lasting contentment."

"Like what—what kind of anchors?" Ryan asks.

"For me it was all kinds of things: Material possessions were the most obvious anchors, a sort of physical manifestation of what was holding me back. But also things like my mortgage, my car payment, most of my bills, and all my debt. Massive, terrible debt. Which I've been chipping away at for a couple years now. And then there were—and still are—other things that are keeping me from freedom, like relationships and my career."

"Your *career*? Really?"

"Really. As well as certain, umm, shitty relationships."

"Shitty relationships? Are you talking about Melissa?[42]"

I smile mirthfully. "You can't change the people around you, but you can change the people around you."

Ryan raises both eyebrows playfully with scorn.

"Some relationships are inimical to our own interests," I say, "and those relationships are anchors."

"How can a relationship be an anchor?"

"Imagine you're in a relationship with someone."

"I *am* in a relationship with someone."

"I know, but for the purposes of my little analogy, let's imagine that you are in a relationship with a hypothetical someone."

"OK."

"Think about how you might've met this hypothetical person—where, under what circumstances, et cetera."

"Alright."

"How did you meet?"

"We probably met at a bar," he says, "or at work."

"Right. A relationship based on convenience and proximity."

"But that's how people meet. We meet at *places*. We say 'Hi, can I buy you a drink?' or 'Hello, my name is Ryan; it's nice to meet you.' It's what we do."

"True, but that way of meeting people is fairly antiquated."

"What's the alternative then?"

"For many years we, along with most of the world, have associated with people based on propinquity."

"Pro-pen-what?"

"Propinquity. Being close to someone or something."

"Oh. Proximity, closeness."

"Correct. Anyway, we've associated with folks based almost entirely on propinquity. In my case, and likely yours too, the people who are closest to me are the people who are, well, *closest* to me. That is, for most of my life I've spent most of my time with people whose largest commonality is proximity: schoolmates, coworkers, acquaintances, networking buddies, and the like."

"And what exactly is wrong with that?"

"It's not about right or wrong. And most of these people haven't been bad people, but other than location, we've had very little in common. We typically don't share similar values or beliefs, and let's face it: values and beliefs are the bedrocks of any meaningful relationship. And in many cases we didn't even share any common interests."

"Interests?"

"That's right, we're not even interested in the same things. Think about the hypothetical woman you met in the bar or at work. What do y'all have in common?"

"I'm not sure."

"Well the only commonalities you can be sure of is that you both like to go to bars, or you both have careers."

"But I don't even really like going to bars."

"Precisely. Plus I know you don't love the work you do. So

your commonalities aren't even things you enjoy, which is how many relationships begin, with little in common, and then we wonder why they don't work out."

"But if we don't meet people at the standard places, then where?"

"I think meeting people should be more deliberate."

"Whadda you mean?"

"This whole minimalism thing has helped me live more deliberately. Accordingly, my relationships are more deliberate too. Besides two of my closest relationships—you and Keri—and a handful of friendships spawned from the corporate world, I've met all my most meaningful relationships online."

"Like, on the Internet?"

"That's right: I've met most of my closest friends on the Internet."

"Living in the future, eh?"

"It's a weird thing to say, for sure. But it's the magnificent truth. And for good reasons."

"But don't you find that the women you date have a problem with your minimalistic lifestyle?"

"Not really. I mean, why the hell would I want to spend significant chunks of time with someone who doesn't share similar values or interests? My lifestyle is predicated on certain principles, and thus my relationships—intimate or otherwise—must align with my own personal standards."

"What if you really like the other person, but they're different from you?"

"Different is great. Sometimes. You see, differences fuel chemistry, and that chemistry makes a relationship exciting; it adds variety. But long term, it's hard to grow with someone if you're both growing in opposite directions, which you will inevitably do if you don't have similar values or beliefs. So you need both: the right balance of differences to keep the relationship from becoming boring, and enough in common that you have a firm foundation."

Ryan nods his head and brushes an invisible piece of lint from his shirt.

"But you see," I continue, "because of the Internet, you and I are no longer relegated by propinquity. We're no longer forced to engage in pointless small talk in an effort to uncover a morsel of commonality. We no longer have to hang out with the guy or gal in the nearby cubicle outside work hours. Instead, we can seek out people with similar values and beliefs."

"Online, you're saying?"

"Yes. The online world has led me to many of my most important relationships. Dozens of people come to mind instantly. I've met a ton of great new friends. And besides friendships, I've also chanced on a few intimate relationships via the 'Net—meaningful relationships that've shaped who I am, that've helped me grow and've allowed me to contribute beyond myself."

"Because of commonalities?"

"Bingo. All my newfound relationships have in common two things: we met because of the Internet, and we see the world through similar lenses. That doesn't mean we always agree on everything, nor do we have the same tastes, opinions, or personalities—we're human beings, not robots, for god's sake—but our common interests allow us to forge bonds that're predicated on something much more meaningful than proximity."

"So how do you meet people on the Internet?" Ryan's interest is clearly piqued.

"I wish there was a simple answer, but because the web is so vast, there's any number of ways to meet new people online. I met Colin Wright via his website. I met my buddy Julien because he and I started exchanging emails about bread."

"Bread? I'm not even going to ask."

"I've met other people on OkCupid or social media. Twitter often works best for me, but there're hundreds of ways to reach out and establish new connections with new people who share your ethics and core behaviors."

I can see the gears turning in Ryan's head. "So the Internet is the place to meet new people?"

"I think so. Although that doesn't mean I think we have to comb only the 'Net to find people who share our morals. But it's important to realize that we're no longer confined by proximity; we're no longer forced to find a soulmate or a friend at the corner bar. We can venture out and find someone who's compatible, someone who's worthwhile. After all, worthwhile interactions make life more meaningful; they make life worth living. Without them, we'd be forced to experience the world with people who aren't understanding or supportive or caring. Or worse, we'd be forced to encounter the world on our own, completely alone, which doesn't sound like a pleasant proposition. Even for an introvert like me."

"I see. What about those *anchors*, though? Those shitty relationships?"

"Because most of the time we develop relationships out of convenience, many relationships are bound to fail."

"That's a strong word—fail."

"Yes but it's the right word. But not just fail in the made-for-TV sense of the word, where two people yell and fight and throw each other's clothes out the window. Rather I mean *fail* as in most relationships are *alright*; they're good, but they're not outstanding. That's because most relationships—the ones predicated on convenience—lack the traits necessary to build a successful bond with another individual, important traits like supportiveness and trust and encouragement. When a relationship is birthed out of convenience or proximity or chemistry alone, it is bound to fail. We need more than a person's physical presence to maintain a meaningful connection, but we routinely keep people around because…well, simply because they're already around."

"I hear you. It's easy to develop a connection with a coworker or a classmate or someone who's always there—even when they're not adding any real value to our lives."

"And it's even easier to stay in those relationships."

"Sure is. Why is that?"

"Because old relationships are convenient, and starting new relationships is difficult—it requires work. But so does anything worth holding on to."

"But sometimes we hold on too long."

"Yep. We've all held on to someone who didn't deserve to be there before. And most of us still have someone in our lives who continually drains us: Someone who isn't supportive. Someone who takes and takes and takes without giving back to the relationship. Someone who contributes very little and prevents us from growing. Someone who constantly plays the victim."

"Victims become victimizers."

"Exactly. And victimizers are dangerous. They keep us from feeling fulfilled. They keep us from living meaningful lives. Over time, these negative relationships become part of our identity—they define us, they become who we are."

"But it's hard to just rid ourselves of negative relationships."

"Hard, yes. But not impossible. We can attempt to fix the relationship, which is obviously the preferable solution. People change over time, and so do relationships. You can change how your relationship works—be it marriage, friendship, or family—without completely ditching the relationship."

"You think so?"

"Yes. It requires sitting down with the person who's draining the energy from your life and explaining to them what must change in order for your relationship to work. Explain that you need them to be more supportive, that you need them to participate in your growth, that they are important to you but the relationship in its current state does not make you happy. Explain that you're not attempting to change them as a person; you simply want to change how your relationship works. And of course ask them what they'd like to change about the relationship. Ask them how you can add more value. Listen attentively."

"What if you're unable to change the relationship?"

"You can end it altogether, which is difficult, but it applies to any relationship: family, friends, lovers, coworkers, acquaintances. If someone is doing nothing but draining your life, it's perfectly acceptable to tell them, 'This relationship is no longer right for me, so I must end it—I must move on.' It's OK to move on."

"Easier said than done," Ryan says.

"Much easier said than done," I agree. "But if you're part of a shitty relationship, you owe it to yourself to move on. You owe it to yourself to be happy with the relationships you have. You are in control. Besides, moving on is sometimes the best way to develop new, empowering relationships. Starting anew, empty-handed and full-hearted, you can build fresher, stronger, more supportive relationships—important relationships that allow you to have fun and be happy and contribute beyond yourself. These are the meaningful relationships we all need."

"What about our own roles in the relationship?"

"Of course it's also important to do your part. Critically important. You too must add value to the relationship. Not by buying gifts or commoditizing your love, but by showing up every day and showing how much you care, demonstrating your love through consistent actions, continually going out of your way to help the other person grow. Both people must do their part to grow the relationship. Only then will both people be satisfied with the relationship they've built."

"So then by getting rid of the anchor of bad relationships, we can develop better ones that better serve us."

"Exactly. Relationships that better meet everyone's needs."

"And so you also said you think your *career* is an anchor?" Ryan asks, sounding more shocked about this than the relationships anchor.

"Yes. It's a huge anchor. It sucks up all my time."

"But you've got a great gig! And you're really good at it."

"No. I have an OK job, one that pays well but doesn't satisfy me. Thanks for saying I'm good at it, but being good at something doesn't mean it aligns with my values. I don't hate my job, but I certainly don't love it. I'm not passionate about what I do."

"Most people would kill for a career like yours."

"That's the problem—it's a career," I say.

"Yeah. So. How's that a problem?"

"Let's take a look at your average day. Your average weekday. How do you spend it?"

"I work like ten or twelve hours a day."

"OK. And what do you call your work?"

"What do you mean, what do I call it?"

"Whatever you do for a living, I think your level of passion can be measured by the label you give your work. People tend to designate one of three labels to their work: job, career, mission. When you speak about your work, which term do you use?"

"I guess I used to have a job when I worked for my dad, back before I joined you in the corporate world," Ryan says.

"Yeah well, a *job* is probably the most common answer—the daily grind. Even people who are unemployed are looking for a *job*. It's a cultural imperative. The American Dream. It's what we're taught to do. We're taught to work senselessly hard in high school and then in college, doing stuff we don't much care about, and then to find a good job, one with reliable pay, good benefits, and maybe a retirement plan if we're lucky. We're taught to work a soul-crushing job for like forty years so that one day we might actually be able to retire and enjoy our lives for like three years."

"Three years?"

"Yes. Not too long ago I saw an insurance-actuary study showing that the average male retiree's lifespan is roughly three years after retirement."

"Shit."

"Shit indeed. We're taught to work foolishly hard for a non-living entity, donating our most precious commodity—our time—for a paycheck."

"Living to work, instead of working to earn enough money to live."

"Precisely. Ultimately most of us come to believe that there's more value in a paycheck—and all the stuff that paycheck can buy us—than there is in life itself."

"But we all need to make money to live."

"No doubt. We all need to pay for a place to live, food to eat, clothes to keep us warm, medical care, and a few other essentials. But this thing everyone calls the American Dream, it's void of meaning. The American Dream is not going to make us happy. In fact, for many people, the pursuit of this set of ideals is oppressive and is guaranteed to be a losing enterprise. And yet we keep looking for better *jobs*."

"But now what I do for a living feels more like a *career*. More adult, mature, grown-up."

"Right. You've worked really, really hard. You've established a career for yourself. I'd posit, however, that a career is one of the most dangerous things you can have if you want to find fulfillment in life."

"That's ridiculous."

"Actually, it's not. Careers are dangerous because people invest so much of themselves into their careers that they establish an identity and a social status based upon where they work and what they do for a living. Think about it: one of the first things a person asks you when you're becoming acquainted is 'What do you do?' On the surface, this seems like an innocent enough question, doesn't it? But the implied question isn't, 'What do you do?' which by itself is rather expansive and could encompass thousands of things: I volunteer at soup kitchens, I work at Walmart, I enjoy fishing on the weekends, I exercise five days a week, et cetera. No, the implied question is 'What do you do for a living?,' 'How do you earn money?,' or just 'Where do you work?' which are all different from the question itself. This supposedly innocent question actually says, 'I will judge you as a person by however you make your money, and I will assign a particular social status to you based on your occupation.' Isn't this one of the first questions you tend to ask other people?"

"It is. Although I've never really thought of it that way, as my identity. But I suppose it sort of is—my job title is a big part of who I am."

"That's because we have to answer this question so often that we've become rooted in our careers—we establish 'what we do' as our core identity, and we give our occupations far more societal worth than they deserve. Once someone establishes their career as who they are as a person, it is hard to shed that identity, even if the person hates their career."

"Yeah, like 'I don't want to work here, but this is just who I am!' I've seen that before. Have seen it in myself from time to time too."

"Thankfully there are better ways to answer the What-do-you-do? question."

"How?"

"I've found that people are programmed to ask this question without giving it any thought. It's not much different from asking, 'How are you doing?' So the best thing to do is to get the other person to actually think about the mindless question they just posited. Whenever I'm presented with this question these days, I tend to answer it by stating what I'm passionate about, instead of spouting off what my vocation is."

"So, instead of saying you're a regional manager or whatever, you say what?"

"I say 'I'm passionate about writing.' and then follow-up that statement with, 'What are you passionate about?' which completely redirects the conversation, changing its trajectory from what you *do*, to what you're both passionate about, which is far more interesting for everyone."

"It definitely sounds more interesting."

"What's even better is that by changing my own thought process around this question, I've been able to move away from that anchor of a career. I've discovered that your life should be your real identity—all the things that interest you, not how you earn a paycheck."

"What are you saying—you might leave Broadspan?"

I look around the stark room as if a secret microphone is planted somewhere. It's a delicate question, with a sort of point-of-no-return answer. Besides the boxes and Ryan and me, the room is vehemently empty, and quiet. I take a deep breath and say, "I don't imagine sticking around much longer. Maybe like five more years. Maybe less."

Ryan's face contorts, miscomputing my words. "But how would you make money?"

"I'm not sure exactly. But then again my relationship with money has changed pretty significantly over the past two years."

"Changed? You still need money, don't you?" Ryan asks.

"Yes, but I don't think about money the same way I used to. For most of my life I thought money was more important than just about everything else. So I sacrificed to make money, and then I sacrificed more to make more money, and then I sacrificed even more to make even more money. You know how it goes: working too many hours, forsaking my health, forsaking the people closest to me, forsaking everything important in pursuit of the almighty dollar."

"Yes. The more things you forsake, the more important the money becomes, because everything else starts to go by the wayside," Ryan says.

"Right. But something is missing in that equation. Obviously. I mean, I make good money—great money—but the problem is that for the longest time I spent even better money. And that was always a serious source of dissatisfaction in my life, one that has haunted me throughout my twenties."

"Those assholes the Joneses are impossible to keep up with."

"Indeed. I was spending more than I was bringing home, and for obvious reasons that equation never balanced, and so money was the largest source of discontent in my life."

"You wasted a lot of money."

"Yeah well, I was stupid. But I wasn't stupid just because I was wasting my income. No, I was far more stupid because of the value

I gave to money. I told myself I was a number, like there was a dollar sign on my head; I could be bought. I told others they could take my time and my freedom in exchange for green pieces of paper with dead slave owners' faces printed on them."

"That's one way to put it. So what changed?"

"I stopped assigning as much importance to money. Sure, I need money to pay for the basics, but I don't need to struggle to earn money to buy crap I don't need anymore. This thing called minimalism has allowed me to get rid of life's excess so I can focus on what's essential."

"Whadda you do differently?"

"Now, before I spend money I ask myself one question: Is this worth my freedom? Like: Is this coffee worth two dollars of my freedom? Is this shirt worth thirty dollars of my freedom? Is this car worth thirty thousand dollars of my freedom? In other words, am I going to get more value from the thing I'm about to purchase, or am I going to get more value from my freedom?

"Sounds like a question worth asking."

"Once I started asking it with enough frequency, it became habitual. I'm a lot less tied to my income now too. I'm not completely out of debt yet, but I've paid off like eighty percent of it—mostly by spending less money. A little something I call the Ramen Noodle Debt Plan."

"Ramen Noodles, eh?"

"It's true. The best way to give yourself a raise is to spend less money. These days I know that every dollar I spend adds immense value to my life. There is a roof over my head at night, the books or the music I purchase add unspeakable value to my life, the few clothes I own keep me warm, the experiences I share with others at a movie or a concert add value to my life and theirs, and a meal from China Garden with my best friend becomes far more meaningful than a trip to the mall ever could."

Ryan gets a bashful grin; a look of thanks forms on his face.

"Basically I no longer waste my money, and so it is far less important to pursue it endlessly. I don't need the same income as I used to."

"But how would you pay your remaining bills? Even if you've reduced your bills, you're still going to have to pay for the basics—rent, utilities, food, insurance."

"I'm not entirely sure. Honestly I'm at a point where I could get by, by working at a coffeehouse if I had to. That wouldn't be ideal, but it'd be exponentially better than working for a corporation whose values don't align with my own anymore."

"So, what then? You want to try to make money doing something you're passionate about?"

"I could try to earn a living as a writer."

"How would you go about that?"

"I'm not sure, but plenty of other people've done it.."

"What if you fail?"

"What if I fail? Like I said, I could always work at the local coffee shop," I say and then it occurs to me to expand on Ryan's question, "That's a good question, though—*what if?* I think we should ask it more frequently. But I think that most of us usually ask *what if?* for all the wrong reasons these days."

"Huh?"

"As kids we used to ask it all the time, right? *What if* we had a treehouse? *What if* we had a trampoline? *What if* we could fly?"

"Yeah," Ryan says with a look of childlike nostalgia.

"We always asked *What if?* with so much optimism, but now the only time we seem to ask it is out of fear."

Ryan uses his teeshirt to wipe sweat from his brow.

"And so we are just dogs, leashed by our own fears," I say,

which sounds much less profound aloud.

"*What if?* has become disempowering," Ryan realizes.

"Yes it has, but it doesn't have to be. We get to choose. So: *What if* I succeed?"

"I like it. So if you decide to be like a full-time writer, how would you go about doing that?"

"I'm not entirely sure, but remember that guy I told you about—Colin Wright?"

"The traveler?"

"Yes."

"What about him?"

"Remember I told you I met with him for lunch this summer?"

"Yeah?"

"Well, we had a long conversation about writing and publishing, and he said I should start a blog."

"What's a blog?"

October evenings tend to show up abruptly in Ohio. It's not even 6 p.m. yet, but daylight has already been drained from Ryan's condo. A streetlight flickers on just beyond the front window, spotlighting a row of mailboxes tucked on the edge of the street. A car drives by slowly, its headlights burning droplets of light rain in its path. A dog barks somewhere out of sight, which scares Ryan's cat and sends him tearing through the house. It's dark in here. The first thing Ryan is forced to unpack from his new collection of boxes is a lamp. Tomorrow is Day One.[43]

7 || Clarity

DECEMBER 2010

If you're driving to Cincinnati at the wrong time of day, a forty-five-minute commute can quickly devolve into a two-hour odyssey. Ohio's two busiest interstates—I-75 and 71—converge and sunder here, making this city a major chokepoint for some of the mindnumbingly worst rush-hour traffic in the country.

This morning is no different. I-75 is a parking lot, encumbered by gridlock and rage. I could literally walk to a hardware store, purchase a sledgehammer, use that sledgehammer to break both of my legs, and still walk to work faster than this. But I wouldn't want to; it's freezing outside and these suit pants are thin.

Over to the east, above Mt. Lookout and Mt. Adams, two of of city's most affluent neighborhoods, it looks like someone ran a giant pink highlighter across the horizon. My car is boxed in by cars on each side of me. Fury seeps from the scowls on every commuter's face within this interstate world. Not me, though. I'm smiling. The last forty-eight hours have been, umm, transformative, for lack of a better term.

In the car to my immediate left, there's a guy maneuvering his jowl's stubble with an electric shaver. To my right, a woman with badly teased blonde hair, wearing a gray blazer, sings along to the radio, which is turned up so loud I can hear John Mayer's "Clarity" through both sets of windows, over the steady hum of my cranked heater. The person in the SUV in front of me—I can't tell whether it's a man with long hair or a woman with short hair—is talking animatedly into his or her mobile phone. It's your standard Friday-morning traffic jam.

The guy in my rearview, however, is a different story—unbelievable, a parody of a haphazard human being. I have to do a triple take when I see him in the driver's seat, a newspaper folded over the wheel, its top fold spilling onto the dash. There is a spoon in his right hand, a bowl of cereal in his left. I've never witnessed someone eat so ferociously. It's like something out of a movie, like he's competing for a prize. Milk drips down his chin with each voracious bite, his shirt and tie somehow untouched by the feeding frenzy. How is he steering?

By the time I get to the office, I'm thirty minutes late, which is a bit incongruent with my first-in-last-out routine.

"You alright?" David, my boss, stops by my office to ask. He's asking not because of my late arrival, but because he actually cares. David McMurry, a friendly, stocky man, not short but not tall, a former pro-tennis player turned executive two-and-a-half decades hence, now in his early fifties, possesses more empathy than most men at his level. He is dressed in vacation colors, wearing one of his casual-Friday buttondowns, a two hundred dollar Tommy Bahama silk Island Shirt. His crow's-feet-framed face is blotched with red, peeking through my office door. He had his first heart attack earlier this year.

"Yes, thanks," I say. My heart starts to speedup to the pace of a two-beat horse trot.

"Not like you to be late," he says without scorn.

"Hey, listen, I finished that reorganizational plan you asked me to put together—"

"Finished it? It's been less than two days. I thought two weeks was pushing it."

"I know, me too. But it's done. Do you have a few minutes?"

He steps into my office and shuts the door and then sits across from me. I can feel the blood pulsing in my left ear, my heartbeat climbing rapidly from trot to canter to full-on gallup.

"You sure you're OK?"

"Yeah. Fine," I say, knowing full well I might pass out.

I hesitate for a few ticks and then slide a simple stack of stapled-together white pages across my desk, nothing as elaborate or as shiny or as professionally bound as one might imagine for a plan with such breadth. Just the facts. The data never lies, does it?

David takes his time, reading each page slowly. The gold Rolex on his left wrist would seem gaudy and ridiculous on almost anyone else, but it fits him; it's as if he's grown into it.

He pauses on page four, labeled TERMINATION LIST in bold, followed by two columns containing forty-two names. He peers over his reading glasses as if they've made the wrong words clear. A look of confusion contorts his features. "Is this some kind of joke?"

Two days ago, on Wednesday December 8, 2010, I received the call from David McMurry. "Part of next year's budget," he spoke in broken sentences, a series of off-beat verbal ticks punctuated by odd pauses. "Eight stores. Forty-two people. Q1. Need a plan in two weeks." It had taken years to learn his choppy, nervous dialect, so I knew what he was saying without need for clarification. Translation: he was giving me two weeks to put together a plan to close eight stores and terminate forty-two people during the first quarter of 2011. On the surface, the logistics for this kind of thing are a nightmare—a sordid cesspool of statistics, graphs exhibiting effects on CapEx and OpEx, employee-ranking hierarchies, all sprinkled with heaps of personal speculation—but this wasn't my first time squeezing into these dancing shoes. I'd been through layoffs before, the bad guy on this side of the corporate table, the man who informs employees, one by one, that they've been downsized or rightsized or outsourced. "Nothing personal," I've said many times, in a tone cultivated to mimic empathy, "we just have to meet the needs of the business." It was never pleasant, but I knew what to do. It's just business.

By the time I got home Wednesday night, it had already been dark for hours. With the blinds drawn and laptop open, I started working up facts and figures for my nothing-personal business plan. But as I did my due diligence, comparing employees to see who was most expendable, something felt different. Something had changed. The actual act of terminating an employee—sitting them down, skimming over the necessary paperwork, having security escort them from the building—had never been easy, but the stats were the stats were the stats. The data was supposed to be easy, objective—the Truth. But it wasn't. No, the numbers could be manipulated, and they painted only a portion of the full picture. Like painting a sunset using only grayscale, it didn't work. These were real people with real lives, men and women with families and mortgages and mouths to feed. And I was going to somehow rank them on a fucking spreadsheet?

Yes, something had changed. Ultimately, that something was…it was me. I no longer bought in to the justifications, to the bullshit mantras, to painting people with statistics. I was tired of the so-called *needs* of the business. None of this was in line with my values or with me as a person anymore. So I let the data fall where it may, choosing which eight stores to close, which employees to give the ax. And then, on page four, right above my forty-one coworkers, I typed one last name at the top of the list: 1. Millburn, Joshua F.

Just a month ago, during his Packing Party, I told Ryan I'd stick around for like maybe another five years, see what happens, you know, schlep my way through the corporate world and maybe save up a little nest egg or whatever. But why wait five more years? I'll be thirty in a few months, and the thought of wasting half the forthcoming decade the same way I misspent the entire past decade seemed not only terrible, but stupid.

This feeling of absolute stupidity—a sort of wiser-man's contempt for his younger self—is probably the closest I've ever come to any kind of epiphany or religious-type out-of-body experience, although I wouldn't classify it as either. Rather, I'd call it *clarity*. For the first time in a long time, things are clear—clearer than they've ever been. I'd been running in one direction as fast as I could, chasing this abstract thing called happiness, but I'd been running the wrong way. I was sprinting east looking for a sunset, when all I really had to do was turn around and walk—not run, just walk—in the other direction.

What Ryan was worried about, though, was my security. Namely, this thing we call "job security," a concept that sends people out of their minds with stress. It's the reason people jump from skyscrapers when they lose their jobs. Not that they're unafraid of jumping—the jump itself is still terrifying—it's just that there's more security in death than in facing the real world and its myriad uncertainties.

And so then we tend to hang on to things—jobs, relationships, material possessions—in an effort to feel secure. But many of the things we cling to in search of security actually drain the satisfaction from our lives, leaving us discontented and overwhelmed.

We hold on to jobs we dislike because we believe there's security in a paycheck. We stay in shitty relationships because we think there's security in not being alone. We hold on to stuff we don't need, *just in case* we might need it down the road in some nonexistent, more secure future.

If such accruements are flooding our lives with discontent, they are not secure. In fact, the opposite is true. Discontent is uncertainty. And uncertainty is insecurity. Hence, by definition, if you are not happy with your situation, no matter how comfortable it is, you won't ever feel secure.

For a dozen years I've blindly embraced the ostensible security of my prestigious career and all the cold trappings of our entropic consumer culture. The super-sized house. The steady paycheck. The pacifying material possessions. I've purchased all the purchases, accumulated all the accumulations, and achieved all the achievements that were supposed to make me feel secure.

So why didn't I experience real security? Why was I glazed with discontent and stress and depression? Because I had more to lose. I constructed well-decorated walls that I was terrified to tear down, becoming a prisoner of my own consumption. My lifestyle, equipped with a laundry list of unquestioned desires, anchored me to my self-built burdens. I thought I knew what I wanted, but I didn't know why I wanted it.

It turned out that my paychecks made me feel *less* secure, afraid I'd be deprived of the income I'd grown accustomed to and the lifestyle I'd blindly coveted.[44] And my material possessions exposed countless twinges of insecurity, leaving me frightened that I'd suffer loss of personal property or that someone would take it from me. So I clutched tighter onto those security blankets. But it's not the security blanket that ensures a person's security. People latch on to security blankets because there's a deeper fear lingering at the ragged edges of a discontented reality; there's something else we're afraid of. The fear of loss. We're afraid of losing love or respect or comfort.

It's this fear that keeps us tied to mediocrity.[45] We're willing to sacrifice growth and purpose and meaning in our lives, just to hold on to our pacifiers, all the while searching all the wrong places for security, misguidedly programming ourselves to believe there's a strange kind of certainty within uncertainty.

But the more we amass—the more we need our stockpile—the more uncertain we feel. Needing more will always lead to a pall of uncertainty and insecurity. Life isn't meant to be completely safe. Real security, however, is found inside us, in consistent personal growth, not in a reliance on growing external factors. Once we extinguish our outside requirements for the things that won't ever make us truly secure—a fat paycheck, an ephemeral sexual relationship, a shiny new widget—we can shepherd our focus toward what's going on inside us, no longer worshiping the things around us.

Sure, we all need a particular level of external security to function: food, water, shelter, clothes, health, personal safety, positive relationships. But if we jettison that which is superfluous, we can find infinite security within ourselves. Security blanket or no, we can be absolutely secure alone in an empty room.

And but then there's the idea of doing something more meaningful with my life. Something I'm passionate about. Although it's usually codified with salient statements of significance

—declarations of "following one's passion," "doing what you're meant to do with your life," or "embracing your true calling"—I simply refer to it as finding my life's *mission*.

That is, I believe everyone has a mission in life. Not the touchy-feely crap promulgated in vapid self-help books, though. I mean, come on, I don't think any of us were "born to do" anything in particular. None of us were born with a preexisting mission. You were not *meant* to do any one thing for the rest of your life.

And yet this idea of birthright mission is promulgated throughout our society, throughout the Internet in particular, as if each person has a preordained vocation that he or she must pursue, as if evolution or natural selection or whatever has spent thousands of years plotting and transmogrifying so that you can be a writer or a yoga teacher or an astronaut.

But life doesn't contain these kinds of absolutes. No one has a predetermined destiny; no one has a singular preexisting mission that is waiting to be uncovered. Truth be told, there are dozens—even hundreds—of things all of us *can* do with our lives, work we can be happy and passionate about. Hence, I think "follow your passion" is crappy advice.

What's important to consider, then, is this question: What is my mission?

Many of us go through life working a job or, worse, a career. We become accustomed to a particular lifestyle, a lifestyle that involves too much spending and personal debt and consumer purchases—our own personalized version of the American Dream. Then we get stuck on the corporate ladder, and before we know it we're too high up to climb down, so high that even *looking* down is a terrifying proposition. So we keep soldiering forward, onward and upward, without ever asking the important questions.

That's not to say that there's anything inherently wrong with working a job; we all have to keep the lights on. But when we travel too far from living a deliberate life (venturing off the path as I have)—and when we stop asking meaningful questions (ditto)—we stop feeling fulfilled.

Like passion, one's mission is not preexisting. And it's not always easy to find or pursue. For me, that means giving this writing thing a shot—finishing my novel and finding a way to get it out to the world. I figure that when you find something—anything—you're passionate about and you make it your life's mission, you will find great joy and reward in the work you do. Otherwise you're just earning a paycheck.

Ultimately, I believe that anyone can be passionate about virtually anything, so long as it aligns with his or her values and beliefs. We're all different; it goes without saying. So just because something sounds banal or boring to one person, that doesn't mean it's not exciting and rewarding for another. It is perfectly plausible to think that someone can be deeply passionate about financial accounting the same way another person might be passionate about, say, horseback riding—neither of which sound too exciting to me, but that doesn't mean there aren't people who're passionate about both.

People occasionally discover a line of work that brings them ultimate satisfaction. Although *discover*, which implies stumbling into, is probably the wrong word. People who do what they love for a living tend to refer to their work as their mission. Not their job, not their career—their mission. Which, as I've said, is cultivated after many hours of doing the work, never simply stumbled upon.[46]

I myself've spent the better part of the last two years cultivating my passion for writing, improving dramatically this year, drudging through the drudgery.

The best writing advice I ever received was from one of my favorite fiction authors, Donald Ray Pollock, a Boomer-generation writer from Knockemstiff, Ohio. (Yes, really—Knockemstiff is a real place, a rough little town in the holler, named after its first bar fight.) Last year, as I started forcing myself to take writing more seriously, I invited Don to lunch so I could pick his brain. My marriage had just ended and I was looking for ways out of the valley.

Sitting at a hole-in-the-wall Thai restaurant in Chillicothe, Ohio, Don bestowed on me his bluecollar brand of downhome Zen wisdom: "There's one secret that's improved my writin' more than anything else." He spoke slowly, with a thicker version of our shared rural Midwestern twang. His accent doesn't make him sound uneducated, quite the opposite actually: it's rough-edged, hard-workin', street smart.

I was perched literally on the edge of my seat, like a child awaiting a magic trick.

"It's so simple it seems dumb to even talk 'bout. But the truth is, well, it has really improved my writin'."

"This ain't some law-of-attraction, spiritual bullshit type of thing, is it?" I asked, accidentally mirroring his infectious dialect, attempting to break the tension with a joke that doesn't land, my timing off beat.

"Nawl," he smiled out of politeness. "And it ain't somethin' you have to learn from years of practicin' neither."

With my ears open, I waited to either accept his sage advice or dismiss it as a writer's bromide.

"My secret is this: I sit in a chair for two hours a day, every day."

"Sit in the chair?"

"That's right. Even if you don't write, hell even when you don't wanna write, plant your ass in the chair e'ery day for a couple hours. Over time, the words will come."

I nodded, taking it in, undecided as to whether his words were profound or platitudinal, though the next year would prove the former to be true. These four words—sit in the chair—ended up becoming an everyday maxim for me, a simple rule that would shape my writing voice over time.[47]

"Make sure you don't have no distractions neither. Just sit in that chair—no Internets, no TV, no radio, no stupid damn phones and tex-mexin'," he said, meaning *text messaging*.[48] "If you're really passionate about writin', you'll do it."

"What about word count? Do you try to write a certain number of pages each day?"

"Oh for Christ's sakes, son. Don't worry 'bout all that shit. You just needah sit in that chair e'ery day without no distractions."

Our food arrived, steaming under the dim restaurant lights. Don is the only man I've ever met who orders steak and potatoes at a Thai restaurant. Over his medium-rare steak and my Massaman curry, he recounted his inspirational story of transition, a story not unlike my own aspirations—he just got started much later in his life than I did.

"What made you want to be a writer?" I asked.

"I'd always been a big reader, all my life. And when I was in my teens I fantasized about writin', thought it'd be a nice way to get by in the world, because, you know, I was pretty naive at the time—thought people could make a livin' at it. I thought writers got to be their own boss and could live anywhere they wanted and that sort of thing. But then life got in the way."

"Life got in the way back in Knockemstiff?"

"Yeah, when I was growin' up there, let's see, I'm fifty-four years old now, so we're talking about the sixties and early seventies,

Knockemstiff was a real community then. You didn't have to go into the city."

For Don, the *city* refers to Chillicothe, a small town in Southeastern Ohio with a population of about twenty thousand.

"There was a general store, three bars, and a church. Pretty much all you need. All that's gone now, though, except the church, and it's damn near a ghost town these days, but back then there was probably maybe five hundred people livin' in Knockemstiff, and I was kin to probably maybe half of 'em."

"Did you start writing when you were young, then?"

"Nawl, I quit high school when I's eighteen and started workin' in factories and ended up with this really good job at the paper mill," he said referring to Mead, which for decades was the largest employer in Southeast Ohio. "It was a union job, paid good money. And so I guess I still had the fantasy in the back of my mind, but I never had the wherewithal or the discipline or nothing to carry it through. Until I was in my forties."

"What changed in your forties?"

"Well when I was forty-five I think I went through this sort of mid-life crisis."

"Same here, except mine was at like twenty-eight."

"I was real disappointed in the way I'd lived my life," he said, a little embarrassment still lingering. "And so I asked myself, What would I want to do with the rest of the time I've got here on earth?"

"We're either living or we're dying, and there is no compensation for approaching death," I said, knowing full well that I wasn't yet living to my fullest abilities either. "So you decided to become a writer as you were approaching fifty?"

"I told my wife I was gonna tryda learn howda write fiction. I told her at the time, 'Hon, I'm forty-five, I'll give it five years, and if nothin' happens by fifty, then I can give myself permission to quit then, and I'll at least be able to say that at least I gave it a shot.' So at the end of those five years I'd published maybe four stories, and I'd also gotten accepted into the MFA program at Ohio State University, and so then I had this decision to make: Do I quit my job and go to graduate school, or do I stay at the mill?"

"Which did you choose?"

"I quit the mill at age fifty. I went to school. Now I don't think anyone has to go to an MFA program to learn how to write; it probably maybe shaved a year off my finishin' that first book though. Getting the feedback, workshoppin' the stories helped a lot, but you don't need no school to do that. Even though I don't really think you can teach someone how to write, the feedback helped a lot. I also learned to be a better reader while I was there—to read different kinds of authors."

"Who were the people you were reading?"

"A lot of different people. When I was forty-five and I first started trying to write, I didn't know what to do. I had no idea howda even start, and what I did for a long time was type out other people's stories on a typewriter."

"I also learned to type on a typewriter."

"Yeah, it was this old IBM typewriter that I had, didn't have a computer at the time, and so you know, I'd type out a story by Hemingway or John Cheever or Denis Johnson. I went the whole gambit, from Richard Yates one week, to Flannery O'Connor the next."

"I thought *Knockemstiff* was very tough and funny when I read it. Hard to believe it's your first book," I said after Don paused to take a bite of cow from his plate. "I saw a few reviews that stressed misery and violence, but the tone isn't miserable; the tone is sort of cheerful, exuberant. It almost seemed like a comic version of the misery of small-town life. And the book certainly ain't violent just for the sake of being violent; if anything it's just real life."

"Well those reviewers probably ain't never been to the holler."

I bobbed my head to show my agreement, realizing that most reviewers hadn't even come close to this world, a sort of north-of-the–Mason Dixon version of the Southern Gothic lifestyle. Don's words felt like they had a double meaning that applied to my life too: life can be shitty, especially in the holler, but you don't have to stay there. You can change. Even a high school dropout—a factory worker from the middle of nowhere—can change. Don's short-story collection went on to be a bestseller, as did his novel, *The Devil All the Time*, and he never went back to the paper mill.

David is still staring at the paper in front of his face, stabbing at my name with his girthy index finger and saying, "Is this some kind of joke?" over and over. The muted winter sun reflects dully off the building outside my office. David's Rolex jangles with each thrust; the paper makes a crinkly sound each time it's speared. He finally sets down the plan and stares over his glasses, not looking *at* me so much as *in* me, looking into the depths of my intentions. I don't know why, but the look in his eyes seems hygienic, cleansed and drained, somehow betraying both disbelief and approval of my foresight all at the same time. The worst is over now. I don't say anything—his question *was* rhetorical, wasn't it?—and instead I sit on my side of the desk, trying hard not to break eye contact while affecting a look that's supposed to look affectless. And then my expression changes, a sort of shrug, as if to say, *If I don't make a change now…then when?* A serious look, although without a mirror I have no idea what my face is doing right now. For all I know I might look like I'm on the verge of a stroke. Inside though, the feeling is different, the strangest mixture of fear and excitement and something else. A nameless thing, as though my stomach has been hollowed out, emptied, and I'm not sure whether it's the bad kind of hollowing out or the good kind. Either that sick-to-your-stomach nausea, or the sort of nauseated feeling you feel after stepping off the most thrilling rollercoaster you've ever ridden. All I can do is sit with this feeling…and wait.

PART TWO || **Remains**

8 || A Well-Curated Life

Sᴇᴘᴛᴇᴍʙᴇʀ 2011

Last night's thunderstorm must've pulled forward this, this sky, clear and blue, deep-blue blue, the same blue as a receptionless digital TV waiting for some kind of input, an empty sky, save only for the flock of blackbirds making a mess of the atmosphere overhead, flying north-northwest, way up past the treeline, the temperature slowly rising with the sun this morning, 8:33 a.m. to be exact, too early for the Midwest's summertime hellfire to've set in, but late enough to be surrounded by daylight, a pleasant, productive time of day, the sun ascending above and behind the westward-facing Newcome Park, which, although the park is situated near the edge of downtown Dayton, barely two blocks from Fifth and Patterson Streets (one of the busiest intersections in the city), the treelined neighborhood itself is muted, hushed but not noiseless, quiet enough that you can actually hear every noise, the tweets and twerps emitting from various species of birds nesting in the trees, the leaves rustling slightly with the wind, a train braying its grave horn in the distance, a car struggling to start and then finally puttering to life directly across the street from my little one-bedroom apartment, nature's own Muzak, everything far enough off the beaten path that I can exercise shirtless here without catching awkward stares, and so I am, in fact, hanging from the monkey bars without a shirt, counting in unintelligible grunts, *nineteen*, *twenty*, *twenty-one*, dressed in logoless black mesh shorts and tennis shoes the color of freshly poured cement, *twenty-three*, *twenty-four*, *twenty-five*, advancing through a series of pullups, my body's motion deliberate, working at a cadence, panting fiercely and letting out controlled babel among the playground's metal fixtures, forced to stop pulling myself toward the playground's equipment at twenty-six and a half, muscle failure, exhausted, worn out, but it's that good kind of worn out, how you feel when your mind and body've synchronized, heart and thoughts pulsing at the same rate, on the same continuum, transcending intention, the soft crunch of mulch underneath my shoe's soles when I drop from the cold iron, a natural brick walkway to my right where I do sets of pushups and squats between intervals of pullups, here alone, basking in solitude, just me and a handful of feral cats who loom through an alley on the northside of the park, the cats protected from the sun by the shade of an 1860s-era brick home whose bricks are regrettably painted fire-engine red, the occasional passerby passing by on foot, which, even though they're almost always inattentive and typing into some sort of handheld device, mesmerized in the glow of their apparatuses, makes the shirtless thing a bit odd at times, not that it actually *is* odd in Dayton, because it's not, at least not anywhere east of the Great Miami River and north of Oakwood, where the de facto dresscode for like ninety percent of guys, beer gut or no, is basically just dusty bluejeans and steeltoe workboots and no shirt, but I'm still a bit self-conscious nonetheless, perhaps unnecessarily so, since I used to weigh two hundred forty pounds at my corpulent zenith, which even at six-two was considerably overweight for me, all belly fat and man-boobs and pale dough-like features, a jowl that was always made worse under the constrains of a necktie and a dress-shirt's buttoned top button, my biceps' skin marked with striated stretchmarks, stretchmarks that're there even now, faded but still lingering, a final fragmentary reminder of my fatter, younger days, a paunchy youth, and so yeah for a long time I've been kind of trepidatious about removing my shirt in public, similar to the fat kid who wears his teeshirt to supposedly protect himself "from the sun" at the local natatorium, even though we all know that the tinted glass ceiling there shields everyone from any skin-burning UVs, and so of course even though I'm down to a healthy one-sixty-five now and've significantly changed my body's size and shape since embracing this whole minimalism thing, eating healthily and exercising each day, alternating among the gym and the park and various at-home exercises mixed with five to ten miles of brisk walking almost every day (weather permitting of course), and now can even see what I think might be (dare I say) my abdominal muscles where a spare tire used to be, but so yes I still think twice before removing my shirt publicly, a flinch that keeps me rooted in the past, a past I'm working hard to untether from, distancing myself from the career and identity that came with it, from all the material possessions I gave so much meaning for so many years, from almost everything that became commonplace during my over-indulgent twenties.[49]

Yeah well yeah so, so I turned thirty earlier this year as the grass darkened to a wet emerald and spring shifted into summer, three decades fading into the background of my life. They say that thirty is the new twenty, but to be honest I'm glad that's not true. I'm happy to face a new decade, moving forward, not backward.

My twenties were my twenties, lost and involuted, but they were not all for naught.

Through my headphones, Nina Simone is crooning the final chorus to "Feeling Good." The door to my apartment is large and blueish black, the color of a healing bruise. The central A/C unit hums its somber baritone inside as the sweat on my face and neck cools and then dries rapidly once it hits the dry indoor air. The building is an old brick house, circa 1880, pre-flood-era Dayton, painted white and converted into three apartments, of which mine is the seven hundred fifty square-foot unit occupying half the second story. At five hundred bucks a month it feels like I'm getting away with some sort of white-collar crime. There's everything I need here: a kitchen with enough kitchenware to host a six-person get-together, which I do from time to time[50]; a livingroom/diningroom with a table and six chairs, a reading chair, and some of my favorite artwork bedecking the walls; a bedroom with a bed and dresser, a desk and chair; and of course a bathroom with everything that's inside a bathroom. The walls throughout are original brick, the floors are wood, and the ceilings are high enough to play basketball should I feel inclined to pick the sport back up.[51]

There are, however, certain things my apartment doesn't have (thankfully): a toaster (I don't eat bread anymore; I opt for unprocessed foods instead); a microwave (I tend to eat fresh foods that don't need to be nuked, using instead my juicer or blender); a television (I stopped watching TV so I could spend that time creating); a couch (which I got rid of recently after realizing I wasn't really using it once the boobtube was gone); too many decorations (now all my artwork is well-curated and unquestionably beautiful (to me), and with less of it, it stands out more, which makes its presence more meaningful, more enjoyable).

I no longer own things that don't consistently add value to my life. I wear all my clothes, use all my dishes, enjoy all my possessions because I've intentionally retained only that which continues to add value. Everything else is gone. We're all different, though, so what adds value to my life might be very different from what adds value to someone else's life.

It is late summer. After submitting my career-suicide plan last December, I was asked to stick around through the transition. So my last day in the corporate world—my point of no return—was February 28, 2011. The first of March was my first day of freedom, which made my insides scream like William Wallace. I've been unemployed for most of this year, and yet I'm not homeless, I'm not starving, I'm still alive. Never happier, in fact. It turns out that happiness suits me.

Take it from me and my first-hand authoritative experience—my empirical evidence, as it were. At age thirty, I earn less money than I did at nineteen, and yet I've never been happier. My happiness is derived from my experiences, from my relationships, from my health—not from my income.

Minimalism has helped me realize that if I relinquish my need for expendable income, and adjust my lifestyle to revolve around experiences instead of material possessions, then I need much less money to live a fulfilled life. As long as I earn enough money to provide my basic needs—rent, utilities, meals, insurance, savings—then I can find my happiness in other ways.

You may've heard the old "burn your boat" parable before, the one in which the warriors arrive on an enemy island and burn their ships as soon as they arrive, which means they are forced to stay and fight; they have no alternative. There's no turning back. They must fight and win or die trying.

In a way, that's what I did when I decided to turn my back on my career—I burned my boat, which at first was terrifying. Even though I knew, intellectually, I'd be fine no matter what happened, I began thinking irrational thoughts, thoughts based on negative, reactionary emotions, like: *What if I end up broke?* and *Will I be homeless?* and *What if I'm not successful at pursuing my passion?* and *What if I'm making a terrible mistake?*

You see, I didn't really have a grandiose plan in which every detail was set and every contingency was outlined. And I certainly didn't have an end goal. Instead, I knew my direction, and I knew how to start walking in that direction.

People have all sorts of clever words to describe what they want to do: objective, target, plan, endgame, outcome, and, of course, *goal*. I, in fact, used to be the Goal Guy in the corporate world. I had financial goals, health goals, sales goals, vacation goals, even consumer-purchase goals. Spreadsheets of goals, precisely tracking and measuring and readjusting my plans accordingly.

These days, life is different; I no longer have goals. Instead of an arbitrary target, I prefer to have a direction in which I travel. If you're searching for a sunrise, it's important to head east. For a sunset, head west.

There was, however, a time in my life when goals were direly important: when I was in a hole and needed to get out. Truth be told, most of my goals were ridiculous and often irrelevant (e.g., purchasing and accumulation goals), but a few of my goals helped immensely (e.g., paying down debt and losing weight). I liken these latter goals to escaping a crater in the middle of the desert. When I was fat and up to my eyeballs in debt, lingering in that bowl-shaped cavity beneath the ground, my goal was to break free from the sun-scorched basin and find the earth's surface. That's because I couldn't even fathom a direction from down there; I simply needed to get out of the hole, and my goals helped me do that.

Once I found the surface, I no longer needed goals. I needed only to look around and pick a direction in which to travel. The nice thing about choosing a direction is that you never know what you're going to get. You might head west in search of the mountains on the horizon but along the way find a beautiful river instead. Or you might traverse the sand dunes only to find a village a few miles from the crater behind you. You never know what's around the bend.

Once I got out of my craters, I didn't need goals to enjoy life. My daily habits helped me do that. Plus, I discovered that it's OK to wander. And if you get lost, so what? I mean, really, would that be so bad? Once you're out of the crater, you need simply to stay out of other craters.

I am *not* a Stoic. And I'm certainly not a Luddite. But I do enjoy conducting little stoical experiments from time to time.[52] Since I left Broadspan earlier this year, I've been testing my limits.

These experiments push me outside my comfort zone, allow me to grow, and force me to learn myriad things about myself. As a result, I've discovered more than I ever thought possible—learning my limits, testing my habits, stretching my mind, confronting my darkest emotions.

The point, however, is not to limit myself. My journey toward a simpler life has never been about deprivation. Rather, I limit myself in the short term so I can learn more about me, learn about my psyche, and ultimately identify what is meaningful in my life.

Often, my post-experiment changes stick; they become

empowering habits that make my life more meaningful. Other times, they don't, but I still gain a deeper understanding of myself.

Thankfully, I've had the opportunity to write about many of these experiments; as of late I've had a venue through which to communicate and express my thoughts and feelings and share my perspective. Four days after setting fire to my boat, Ryan and I took Colin's six-month-old advice, and together we (Ryan and I) started a website. We called it *TheMinimalists.com*.

Ryan, looking through his Packing Party notes, realized two things: (1) we're not crazy,[53] and (2) this minimalism thing has the potential to not only add value to *our* lives, but to other people's lives too. "Who knows," Ryan said to me, "people might find value in our separate—appreciably different—journeys."

Around the same time, through my own reflection, I learned about something I call *Transference*—leveraging one's current skillsets and transferring those skills to new endeavors. There are certain skills and passions that I had cultivated over the years— namely writing fiction and coaching employees—and that if I tweaked those talents slightly, I could combine my abilities to contribute to my little corner of the world in a greater way.

And so together, amped up on excitement and caffeine, Ryan and I wrote a few dozen essays. Even though we had no idea what we were doing, we were able to cobble together a basic website.[54] And we even had our buddy Adam, an amateur photographer from Cincinnati, take photos so we wouldn't look like criminals when we pasted our goofy mugshots on the web. Voila! *The Minimalists* was born on December 14, 2010.

So there we were, our story dangling from the Internet's rafters for the world to see…and judge. It was exhilarating and terrifying at the same time.

Then something remarkable happened: fifty-two people visited our website in the first month.[55] Fifty-two! That might sound unremarkable at first, but it was the first time anyone had read my words without sending me a rejection letter. The feeling alone almost made me foam at the mouth with excitement.

And then other remarkable things happened: fifty-two readers turned into five hundred, five hundred become five thousand, and now more than a hundred thousand people show up to read our words every month.

I didn't plan on this. I figured I could skate by writing fiction and working part-time until I made enough money to just write. But it turns out that when you Add Value to people's lives, they are eager to share the message with friends and family. People are intrinsically wired to share value with others. Adding Value is a basic human instinct.

It all seems rather overnightish, I know. But it wasn't. There's no hidden secret—no quick fix—when it comes to *The Minimalists*' growth. In retrospect, it's actually pretty simple to dissect—and it's the opposite of what you might think.

These days, everything is purportedly easier than ever. The quick fix is the new black. It's in vogue. Everyone wants it—the overnight success, the secret formula, the magic pill. The path of least resistance is endemic in our current culture. We all want to Go Viral. But *why*? Is there a reason we try to create the viral video, the over-shared blog post, the retweeted tweet? Or are we all just Pavlov's dogs, drooling on command for a morsel of attention?

Whatever the reason, Going Viral seems to be a sign of the times. Everyone is striving for Warhol's prophetic fifteen minutes of pseudo-fame, attempting to aggregate as many eyes as possible in their direction. We have moved past the Information Age and stumbled face-first into the Overcommunication Era. In the past, we all wanted to be liked; now we just want to be "Liked."

More than a decade ago I was dragged to a party on a college campus where I came across a preposterous sign hanging in a dorm bathroom. It commanded in a bold typeface that all men should "Please masturbate in your own rooms!" I guess they had a problem with guys whacking it in the showers.

Fast-forward ten years, and that sign is an appropriate metaphor for today's masturbatory Internet culture. Many of us get so caught up in displaying ourselves online that we are willing to do just about anything to Go Viral. It's not hard to find; just take one glance at your Facebook feed—*Hey look at me! Look what I'm doing! I'm so sad/happy/excited! Pay attention to me!* Crowds of people are congregating, shouting against the never-ending spill of digital noise.

When our shouting doesn't work and the noise becomes too loud, we resort to silly stunts and obscene displays of self: the drunken videos, the melodramatic posts, the shirt-off-in-the-mirror photos, the pop-up ads and sleazy act-now marketing, the superfluous cursing in forums (don't even get me started on YouTube comments). Sure, yelling loudly enough will attract scads of newcomers—we can't help but slow down and gawk at the wreckage, but we never stick around to watch the post-accident cleanup. Similarly, someone's public indecency—his or her viral missive—may draw some initial head-turns, but when everyone leaves the scene of the accident, Mr. Viral will be left feeling empty and alone.

Why would I want to Go Viral anyway? The word itself literally means "caused by a virus"? Last time I consulted a Physician's Desk Reference, a virus was a bad thing—an infection, a disease, a harmful or corrupting influence.

Maybe I'm allergic to the magic pill, but Ryan's and my own overnight success didn't happen, umm, overnight. As far as I can tell, Viral content is but a well-crafted soundbite, devoid of substance. So instead of Going Viral, I focus on one thing: Adding Value. These two words regularly pop their beautiful little heads into my daily conversations. Habitually, before every tweet, every status update, every essay I write, I ask myself, *Am I Adding Value?*

Adding Value surely doesn't sound as sexy as Going Viral, but it's the only way to gain long-term buy-in, and it's one of the few ways to build trust. When people trust you, they are eager to share your message with the people they love. Contribution is a basic human instinct; we are built to share value.

I understand that Ryan's and my (or any other successful person's) seemingly rapid rise from obscurity might *seem* rapid—at least from the other side of the glowing rectangle. But what you see is only the end result. Before your favorite rock stars were headlining festivals and stadiums around the world, they had to earn the calluses on their fingertips. What you perceive as overnight success is, in fact, everything *after*—after the tedium of repeated failures, after the monotony of writing twelve hours a day, after drudging through the drudgery, after adding value to one, two, ten, hundreds, and then thousands of people's lives. What you see is the culmination of years of hard and steady work. There's nothing overnight about it.

As our website grew, so did the number of my burgeoning personal experiments. My first experiment shocked many of my Midwestern friends: I got rid of my television. Why? Because I watch it. A lot.

You see, I sort of enjoy television. It's easy to watch. It's passive. It's quite entertaining at times. And I don't have to do much work when you're basking in its warm glow.[56] But there's no reward emitting from the glowing box. Ultimately, the overarching costs of television drastically outweigh the benefits....

Money. A television itself can cost hundreds or even thousands of dollars. Plus, there're the monthly costs of cable or satellite (and all the little extra fees for cable boxes, DVRs, HD service, premium channels, etc.). There're the movie rentals or purchases, many of which we don't even watch. And there're all those ancillary items we think we need: the surround-sound system, the multi-disc Blu-Ray player, and don't even get me started on video games; that's an entirely different—and equally troubling—story.[57] But TV costs us a lot more than money.

Time. TV viewing has robbed me of my time—my most precious asset. Even with the Internet, the average person watches greater than five hours of TV each day. Imagine what I could create with an additional thirty-five hours a week of free time.

Attention. Sometimes I'd trick myself into thinking I was "multi-tasking" by doing other things while watching the tube—folding laundry, responding to emails, writing a story. Deep down, though, I know I'm not able to focus my attention on several things at once without drastically reducing the quality of the finished work.

Awareness. Awareness is the most precious kind of freedom. We should cherish it. But TV often makes us oblivious to the world around us. And so, in a roundabout way, TV has siphoned off my freedom.

Relationships. If I'm watching TV alone, I'm withdrawing from my relationships with other people. Television can erect a barricade that defends us from everything we don't want to keep out: love, connection, intimacy, friendship.

Creativity. If we are constantly consuming, we are not creating. Hence, TV has the ability to purloin our creativity.

I don't, however, think anyone has to chuck their TV out the window to be a minimalist. They don't. There are ways to use it more deliberately, though: For example, Ryan disconnected his cable service, got rid of his DVDs and video games, and still kept his TV for occasional viewing. Or, sometimes I schedule time to watch TV with other people; I don't do it often, but if I want to watch a TV show or movie, I can watch it at someone else's house, and we can discuss it afterward. This type of planned viewing is less passive and helps us build and strengthen relationships, rather than take away from them. I know other people who've kept television and cable in their homes but've gotten the glowing box out of their bedrooms. I mean, as far as I'm concerned, a bed has only two purposes anyway, neither of which include watching latenight reruns.

Next, as 2010 faded into 2011, I stumbled into my first ever New Year's resolution: I set out to purchase zero material possessions all year.[58] To be honest, I've always thought New Year's resolutions were kind of dumb, and so I didn't realize how difficult this would be. Alas, it was difficult—very, very difficult. But it was worth the difficulty: within two months my entire thought process around consumer purchases changed significantly.

At first, whenever I was faced with a retail establishment's massive shelves and all its consumer-product offerings, I'd think, *Hey, look, that thing looks cool—I think I'll buy it.* That is, my natural impulse was to purchase. To buy. To accumulate. To acquire. To own. To possess. But eventually, I was forced to face the fact that I couldn't buy those things, reminding myself each time of my commitment not to purchase.

By the end of April something beautiful had happened: I no longer wanted to buy new things. I had accidentally reprogrammed myself; my entire thought process around impulse consumption had changed. Sure, the whole point of my resolution was to prove I didn't need to buy stuff for a year, but I learned that I could actually change *myself* in the process. After four months, I no longer wanted to buy stuff on impulse. The endless desire to consume was gone. It was—and still is—a phenomenal feeling.

But then, six months into the experiment, an unfortunate thing happened: I spilled tea on my computer. Not just a little. An entire cup, all over the keyboard. It was ruined. Thankfully, my first thought was not, *I guess I'll go buy another computer.* Instead, I thought, *How can I find a way to live without this item?*

I went the next few weeks without a computer. I wrote essays longhand on legal pads. I wrote fiction by hand which looked like the musings of a madman. I accessed the internet at libraries, at friends' houses, anywhere except my tea-soaked laptop.[59]

Eventually, Ryan offered to buy me a new laptop for my thirtieth birthday—an offer I turned down because I felt like that was cheating. So I soldiered on, computerless for several more weeks.

A month in, though, I realized I was less productive without my computer. I was writing less, I wasn't enjoying writing as much, and I didn't feel as good about what I was writing. I realized I was depriving myself of an essential tool. For me, a computer was essential, so I got a new one. But I never went back to my impulse-driven consumption of yesteryear. At the end of the day, I guess you could say my resolution failed. But it was a beautiful failure, one that doesn't feel like failure at all.

Then, when I moved into this smaller apartment—the one I'm standing in right now, post-workout—I realized I wasn't as productive as I'd've liked, so I decided to forgo home-Internet access for thirty days, just to see what'd happen.

It turns out that killing the Internet at home was the best decision I've ever made with respect to productivity.

No longer am I caught in the Web at my home. Because I must *plan* my Internet use, I'm forced to use the Internet more deliberately. If I see something I want to research on the Web, I can't just jump at the impulse; I have to write it down and use that list during times of connectivity. Which also means I'm forced to leave the house to access the 'Net. So I go to the library or to a coffee shop or some other place with free WiFi, grab a cup of coffee or tea, and do all the stuff I need to do online (publish writing, check email, read blogs, etc.). Because I'm out of the house and people are around, I also get to meet new people; it just so happens that I've met several new friends this way, which is a hell of a bonus.

I know what you're thinking, so let me address it now. You're thinking: *But you're a writer, Joshua, and that's why it made sense for you!* And you're also thinking: *I need the Internet for homework/work-work/Netflix/online dating/online gaming/updating my Facebook status/playing Farmville/surfing eBay for shit I don't need/stalking my high school boyfriend/etc./etc.* Maybe you do. But are you certain? Because maybe you don't. What would happen if you didn't have Internet at home for a month?[60]

Now when I'm on the Web, it has a purpose—it's a tool I use to enhance my life. Sure, sometimes I log on and watch funny videos or goof around on social media, but I go to the Internet with the intention of doing these silly things—I give myself permission to slack off from time to time. Even my slacking off is more deliberate.

When I decided to relinquish home Internet, I did it mostly so

I could focus on writing without distractions. But I found so many additional benefits too: My time at home is more peaceful, a personal sanctuary. My thoughts are clearer, less fragmented. And perhaps most important, I find myself doing more meaningful things with my time: reading, writing, thinking, exercising, walking, spending time with friends.

Because my no-Internet experiment was easier than I thought, I started feeling brave, and so I figured: *Why not get rid of my mobile phone for a couple of months and see what happens?*

Going without a phone for any extended period of time seems to be the modern-day equivalent of a vow of silence. But when I decided to 86 my phone for sixty days as an experiment just to see whether or not my world would keep spinning, people were shocked. Some people were appalled. Some were downright worried about me. Which invites a question: must one unplug from reality to properly observe reality?

I'll abstain from overused *Matrix* references about unplugging from the grid and simply say that I learned more about myself than I intended. I couldn't've done so without disconnecting for a while, without stepping back and actually thinking about my life in a deliberate, uninterrupted way.

I learned…

That we have weird expectations. I realized I needed to get rid of my phone for a while when I felt pressure to respond to text messages, email, and social media throughout the day. You might expect someone to respond to a text message in an hour; someone else might expect a response in ten minutes; another person might expect a response the same day. These expectations are arbitrary. When I eliminated my ability to respond immediately, I was able to toss everyone's expectations out with the bathwater.

That without the vapidity of ephemeral text conversations, my real face-to-face conversations have became more meaningful. I spend more time listening, giving my full attention to the conversation at hand. As a result, I enjoy these conversations more.

That people are generally supportive and understanding. When we make changes in our lives, we're often afraid of what people will think of us. Will they think I'm crazy or stupid or out of touch? The truth is, people are more supportive and understanding than we think. Particularly the people who are closest to us. Especially when we discuss our changes with them and let them know we're making the changes so we can live happier lives.

That we subconsciously program ourselves. Without knowing it, our daily activities have a profound impact on our future selves. I used to reach for my phone every few minutes no matter where I was—even at the urinal. Even when the phone wasn't with me I would reach for it. I was programmed to do so. I call this the Twitch.

That we can reprogram ourselves. Similarly, we can change our patterns. When we remove a habit from our lives, we become acutely aware of how that habit affected us. This is true for any habit: smoking, over-eating, etc. It took twenty-two days for me to reprogram the Twitch, twenty-two days of pausing and noticing why I was Twitching. After twenty-two days, though, I no longer felt the urge to immediately react; I no longer felt the need to pacify myself with transitory activities like texting or responding to emails during every moment of "downtime."

That "downtime" is a misnomer. Human beings used to have precious interstitial zones in which we could find momentary solace: airports, checkout lines, waiting rooms, and other places were transient sanctuaries in which we could bask in reverie. This is no longer the case.[61] I now notice everyone on their phones during these precious moments. They are attempting to be more productive or interactive, but I've discovered that stopping and thinking during these moments is more productive than fiddling with my phone.

That the world goes on. Without a mobile phone, without the Internet, without a TV, the world keeps turning.

That you can test anything for a short period of time to see whether it's right for you.

That it's not that hard to give up anything when you live in the real world.

That, in all honesty, there wasn't a single time when I actually *needed* my phone during my two months without it. Sure, there were times when it was inconvenient, times when I had to fight through the frustration, but that was a small price to pay to reprogram the Twitch. Yes, I'll go back to using a mobile phone for practical purposes—GPS, necessary phone calls, the dictionary app I missed dearly—but I'll use it differently going forward. I'm not going to use it to check email anymore; I'm not going to use it to send text messages while driving or standing at a urinal; and I'm not going to rely on it as my primary means of interacting with the world around me. My usage will be more intentional than it was before; my phone will be a tool, not an appendage.

Amongst all the growth through experimentation, through all the personal investigations, I decided that one more thing had to go: come June 2011, I elected to rid myself of (gasp!) my goals.

The corporate mantra by which I lived for a decade-plus was *You can't manage what you don't measure*. It sounds good, but the problem with this catchphrase is that it's total bullshit. We used to measure *everything* at Broadspan. There were twenty-nine metrics for which I was responsible every single day (even on weekends). There was morning reporting, 3 p.m. updates, 6 p.m. updates, and end-of-day reporting. Suffice it to say, I was consumed by numbers. I thought and dreamed in spreadsheet terms.

But then I realized something: It didn't really matter. The goals were never as powerful as someone's internal motivations. You see, people work hard for two reasons: they are externally inspired to do so, or they are internally motivated to do so. Sometimes it's a combination of both. Sure, some people can be momentarily inspired by goal attainment, but that kind of inspiration doesn't last beyond the goal itself.

Conversely, intrinsic motivation—such as the desire to grow or contribute—carries on long after the goal is met. External inspiration can be the trigger, but internal motivation is what fuels one's desire. Thus, when you discover your true motivation, you don't need an arbitrary goal.

Ergo, I have lived the last hundred days with no goals.

When I had the opportunity to meet Leo Babauta four months ago during a trip to San Francisco, he said there were three things that significantly changed his life: establishing habits he enjoyed, simplifying his life, and living with no goals.

I was already living the first two: I had established pleasurable habits, and I had simplified my life. But it was difficult for me to grasp the "no goals" thing. The thought of living a life with without goals sounded insane to me—it was counterintuitive, it was scary, it went against almost everything I had ever learned about productivity. I needed a way to quit my goals cold turkey, so I did two things after speaking with Leo.

First, I asked myself, *Why do I have these goals?* I had goals so I could tell whether I was "accomplishing" what I was "supposed" to accomplish. If I met a goal, I was allowed to be happy—right? Then I thought: *Wait a minute, why must I achieve a specific result toward an arbitrary goal to be happy? Why don't I just allow myself to be happy now?*

Second, I decided to live with no goals for a while. I didn't know how long, because I didn't make it a goal. I figured I'd give it a shot for a month or so, maybe longer, to see what happened. If it affected me negatively, I could return to my rigid life of "achieving" and "producing results" with my color-coded spreadsheets containing scads of goals.[62]

I didn't need to go back, though. Breaking free from goals changed my life in at least three ways.

First off, I am less stressed. People who've known me for years comment on how calm I am. With no goals, they say I'm a noticeably different person—a better person.

Second, I am more productive. I didn't anticipate increased productivity in my post-goals life. If anything, I thought getting rid of goals meant I was going to sacrifice results and productivity. But the opposite has been true. I tossed the idea of productivity and became more productive as a result: I've written the best fiction of my life. I've watched our website's readership increase significantly. I've met remarkable new people. And I've been able to contribute to other people like never before. The last hundred days have been the most productive days of my life.

Third, I am happier. During my thirty years on this earth, I've never felt this type of intense contentment. With the decreased stress and increased productivity resulting from no goals, I am able to enjoy my life; I am able to live in the moment without constantly planning for my next accomplishment.

During this no-goals experiment, three good arguments

against the no-goal lifestyle presented themselves to me, all three of which I'd like to address:

Complacency: Doesn't a life with no goals make you complacent? Well, if by "complacent" you mean "content," then yes. But, otherwise, no. In fact, the opposite was true: after removing the stress from my life, I partook in exciting new endeavors that I likely wouldn't've attempted under goal's regime.

Growth: Doesn't a life with no goals prevent you from growing? No. I've grown considerably in the last hundred days. I've gotten into the best shape of my life, strengthened my personal relationships, established new relationships, and written more than ever. I've grown more than any other hundred-day period.

You still have goals: You say you have no goals, but don't you still have some goals, like finishing your new novel or "being happy" or "living in the moment"? It's important to make a distinction here: Yes, I want to "be happy" and "live in the moment" and "live a healthy life," but these are choices, not goals. I choose to be happy. I choose to live in the moment. I choose to live a healthy life. I don't need to measure these events; I simply live this way. As for the novel I've been working on, I intend to finish writing it. I've never worked harder on anything in my life, but I'm enjoying the process of writing it, and if I never finish, that's OK too. I'm not stressed about it anymore.

Living with goal-less has changed my life, adding layers of happiness I didn't realize were possible. I'm don't see any reason to retreat back to a goal-oriented life. No more goals for me. My life is better without them.

Goal-less, TV-less, Internet-less, and phone-less, I've recently embraced another experiment: minimalist exercise. I've come to learn that no amount of money will buy me better habits; no fancy gym membership will whip me into better shape; no expensive equipment will make me exercise more. So I exercise only eighteen minutes a day, alternating between pushups, pullups, and squats until I'm tuckered out.

Like writing, I had put off my health for so long. A couple years ago, I was the successful suit-'n'-tie guy who couldn't do a single pushup. Hell, I didn't exercise at all. Or, when I did exercise, it was sporadic; it never lasted more than a few days before I gave up. Even after losing seventy pounds—which was almost entirely due to diet[63]—I was in terrible shape. At age twenty-eight, I was doughy and flabby and weak. But not anymore.

At age thirty, I'm in the best shape of my life. That's a weird thing to say, I know—but it's the truth. I'm in good shape because I've found ways to enjoy exercising; I've found ways to make exercise a daily reward instead of a dreaded, tedious task.

What has changed? I do only exercises I enjoy. For instance, I don't enjoy running, so I don't do it. I attempted it for six months and discovered it wasn't for me. If you see me running, call the police, because someone is chasing me.[64] Instead, I find other ways to do cardio: I walk or do bodyweight exercises that incorporate cardio.

Although I enjoy exercising most in the mornings, I love hitting the park in the evenings if I feel tense. Exercising at the end of a long, stressful day provides me with time in solitude to reflect on what's important.

Moreover, variety keeps exercise fresh. When I first started exercising, I used to hit the gym three times a week, which was certainly better than not exercising at all. Then, as I got more serious, I started going to the gym daily, which became time consuming. Plus, doing the same thing over and over eventually caused me to plateau. These days I mix it up: I walk every day, and I still go to the gym occasionally, but the thing that has made the most noticeable difference has been the variety of my daily eighteen-minutes.

Yes, I know, eighteen minutes sounds like an arbitrary number—that's because it is. When I started my bodyweight exercises, I didn't have a specific window of time in mind. But I timed myself for a week and discovered that almost every time I visited the park for my workout, I was worn out within eighteen minutes.

I don't have a specific routine or plan, I simply take a thirty-second break between sets, bouncing from one exercise to the next. After eighteen minutes, I'm spent. Every tedious task typically associated with exercise—driving to the gym, waiting around to use the weights, etc.—is gone. Now with everything out of the way, exercise is exhilarating. Plus, I don't have any more excuses. I mean, everyone has eighteen minutes a day to focus on their health, right?

With each and every experiment I've felt as if I was reprogramming a long-ago-programmed Twitch. Addition by subtraction. By getting rid of my expectations, my programmed actions, my misconceptions, I've changed myself. I've discovered that growth happens most rapidly whenever I step into my discomfort zone.

That is to say, I don't do things I dislike, but I do do a lot of things that force me to feel discomfort. If I dislike an activity, I find a way to unfasten it from my daily life. But I also place myself in uncomfortable situations that help me grow.

The difference, then, has to do with timing. When something is new and unfamiliar, it is by definition not natural, not comfortable. In the long run, though, I don't keep drudging through tasks I don't enjoy. Even with seemingly mundane tasks like folding laundry or cleaning the house, I either find a way to enjoy it (folding laundry is actually meditative for me), or if I absolutely dislike it, I'll hire someone to do it for me, while I move on to something new. Life is too short to do shit you dislike.

So far this morning I have written for three, maybe four, hours, and then I read for half an hour, followed by the simple exercise regimen I just finished. I don't have a daily routine, though; I no longer need one. I do, however, have habits on which I focus every day. Don't get me wrong, I used to have a routine. In fact, most of my adult life has been plagued with repetition. And I hated that routine. Every day felt like Groundhog Day: awake to a blaring alarm, shower, shave, put on a suit and tie, spend an hour or more in mind-numbing traffic, succumb to the daily trappings of emails and phone calls and instant messages and meetings, drive home through even more mind-numbing traffic, eat a frozen dinner, search for escape within the glowing box in the living room, brush my teeth, set the alarm clock, sleep for five or six hours, start all over again before sunrise.[65]

That was life most days. The same thing over and over. And then last year when I decided it wasn't for me anymore, I canceled my routine. Or rather, I traded in my routine for better habits.

Hence, it's not even nine o'clock and I've already done a lot today, and yet there's still an entire day ahead of me. My secret? I don't do much. Seriously. Sure, it seems like I do a lot of things, but I don't. My experiments have allowed me to develop habits I enjoy, while limiting my distractions.

To put it simply, I am more productive by doing less. Rather than the normal productivity tropes of planning and scheduling, attempting to force production, I get more done by focusing on only the important stuff first, working through the tasks that truly matter, embracing Real Priorities instead of engaging in fluid inactivity.

Usually that means doing things that're more difficult than I'd like. For me, writing is difficult, exercise is hard, even reading is not passive. Virtually everything that's meaningful—everything worth doing—requires a good amount of effort. But of course that's where all the reward is.

Likewise, the passive tasks—Facebook, email, television, etc.—are easy. And they are fine in small doses (I'll likely check my email for thirty minutes today or tomorrow, and I'll certainly spend a few minutes on Twitter). But there's no grand reward for passivity, just pain and regret and an emptiness that's hard to articulate.

Later today I'll walk five or ten miles, wandering the streets of Dayton (another form of meditation, contemplation mixed with physical activity); I'll meet with Ryan to discuss an essay we're working on; and I'll spend some focused dinner-and-conversation time with my girlfriend, Colleen, whom I met earlier this year. She'll look at me ruminatively, with locks of curly hair framing her pretty face, and she'll ask me about my day; I'll ask her about hers, and I'll listen. Like really, really listen. Pay attention. Be there with her. Just *be*.

These days, my life is filled with these *active* activities, each of which requires more effort from me than the boobtube, though they all have exponentially higher payoffs.

Ryan is late again.[66] David Gray's "Please Forgive Me" is playing softly on the radio in my apartment. There's an early evening moon outside that looks half-eaten. I see Ryan scurry to my door with the focus of someone who should be on ADHD medication. I'm supposed to meet my girlfriend in less than ninety minutes. Ryan is on his phone, and before he makes it to my door he rushes back to his car to get something he forgot.

This evening we're supposed to catch up for an hour over tea and blank pages. He's rushing back toward my apartment now. Through the window, I see him hang up his phone, and I open the door before he has the chance to knock. A week from today he will receive the news that Broadspan has made him redundant—he's been rightsized, laid off. Because he too has been planning a new future, he'll inform me that, although it's scary, being laid off is the best thing that's ever happened to him.[67]

9 || Harvest Moon

Ocтober 2011

Colleen and I are driving west, enveloped by sprawling cornfields on both sides of this two-lane county road. Having just witnessed a buttery sunset melt into perfect rows of tall, Midwestern cornstalks that stretch beyond the horizon, we are now surrounded by twilight, that thin sliver of time between the bustle of the day and the calm of the night. The sky is so clear overhead I could point out various constellations through the sunroof.[68]

With no real destination in mind, my left hand is gripping the steering wheel while my right rests on Colleen's knee. Our post-sunset world is silent except for the hum of the road and the background radio playing a song by the Black Books, an indie band she used to hang with during her art-school days in Cleveland. Colleen turns up the volume and sings along: "If you're not sunburned, you're not having fun."

Today is the second Tuesday in October; Southwest Ohio's Indian summer is coming to a close. And even though we're not sunburned, she and I, we *are* having fun—golden tan after a summer spent playing outdoors together, running through sprinklers and gamboling amid treelined parks and doing all the cliche things young couples do when they're falling in love. It feels wonderful to be together, alive together, alive, together.

Dancing like a jellyfish in a summer dress, Colleen is belting out off-key lyrics from the passenger seat. It doesn't matter that she's off key, though; her singing seems perfect anyway. I can't help but look over from the driver's seat, to steal glances every chance I get, removing my eyes from the road just to take her in.

Colleen is the prettiest girl I've ever met. I know that sounds hyperbolic, and you're probably not going to believe me, but whatever. Whether you believe me or not, it's simply the truth. She's beautiful. Big glacial-blue eyes. Crazy, curly, honey-colored hair. Her perfect smell, a sweet mixture of sweat and shampoo. And that...that...that smile. God that smile. I couldn't describe it without stealing hackneyed lines from Keats's poems. Hell, even the scar on her chin seems to be in the right place.

When we met earlier this year, I was walking into my thirties, my twenties fading into memories. Not too surprisingly, we came into contact via the Internet, after she sent me a clever and silly Tweet about meeting for "decreasingly warm liquids.[69]" Although she is two years younger than I am, Colleen is the one who's helping me learn what it means to be in love. Of course she's not perfect, but she's the closest thing I've ever witnessed: honest, vulnerable, openhearted. Around her I want to be a better version of myself, the *best* version of myself. For the first time in my life I feel uxorious.

"Why haven't they harvested all this yet?" I ask, sweeping my hand from left to right to indicate a profusion of unreaped crops on the other side of the windshield. The earth around us is swollen with corn, corn in every direction, corn out every window, more corn than you can imagine. It's literally unimaginable.

"Hell if I know," Colleen says playfully, contorting her face a bit. "Who do I look like, Old McDonald?"

"Oh come on, ain't you and your people from 'round these parts?" I say. We are near a small farmtown called Greenville,[70] roughly twenty-five miles north of Dayton, about fifteen miles east of the Indiana state line.

"What you mean, *you people*?"

I can't help but smile with a face full of mirth, a smile I'd probably make fun of if it wasn't my own goofy, love-struck grin.

"What the fuck[71] is that?!" Colleen shouts from out of nowhere.

"What? Where?" I ask, nearly driving off the road with sudden terror, peering in the wrong direction like an idiot.

"That! What is that?" she nudges me to look northwest. Her face is lit like an excited child's. Beyond a lattice of cornstalks, it appears as if the sun is somehow reemerging on the horizon, a huge blood-orange disc aflame and ascending over Darke County. It isn't until we pull to the side of the road and roll down the windows that we realize it is in fact not the sun but the moon, the brightest moon either of us has ever witnessed.

We are stuck in our own stares. A breeze catches the fields beneath the bright moon, making the crops look and sound like ocean waves through our rolled-down windows. Everything feels sort of like a David Lynch film—realistically surreal, pleasantly distended. The stars blur. The locusts' chirrs echo. Colleen's wide-eyed laughs hang in the air, suspended in a frozen moment. It all seems too good to be true, a rare perfect moment, an *us* I never expected, seemingly irreplicable.

Of course the following months will produce countless wonderful moments like this, revealing what it feels like to be truly free, producing the happiest days of my life thus far. And yet somehow I will manage to fuck it up. Three seasons from now, as spring bleeds into summer, as I focus more on blind achievement, as I focus on my new online life and turn a blind eye to the world around me, as I lose my awareness of what's real, I will complicate a love that was so simple. Eventually, after our relationship's light has dimmed, Colleen and I will part ways, and I will learn another important life lesson: when you stop paying attention to everything that's important, when you lose sight of the happiness that's right in front of your face, when you search for it through supposed accomplishments and accolades and recognition, it's not appreciably different from searching for happiness through material things. Happiness doesn't work that way. When the pursuit is ill-conceived, life loses its magic, loses its purpose, and you lose everything that matters. The truth is, you can skip the pursuit of happiness altogether and just be happy.

After my failure, in the wake of the damage done, I will spend months peering into the heartbreak gulf that separates Colleen and me. In time, after much reflection and countless tears, I will be able to look over my shoulder and see where I went wrong....

Every relationship—friendship, romantic, or otherwise—is a series of gives and takes. Every relationship has an Us Box. For the relationship to work, both people must contribute to—and get something from—that Us Box. If you just give but don't get, you'll feel used, exploited, taken advantage of; and if you only take but don't give, you're a parasite, a freeloader, a bottom-feeder.

Throughout most of our year together, Colleen and I both contributed significantly to our Us Box. We gave and gave and gave. Consequently, our love multiplied, and we each got out way more than we put in. It was beautiful, by far the best relationship of my life. We each contributed, and we both grew—we grew together. But a year into our love, I began to feel stagnant, as if I was no longer growing, and I wasn't sure why. So I unintentionally built walls while I attempted to figure out my stagnation.

But in reality, I wasn't growing as much as I once was because I was no longer contributing as much as I once was. While Colleen continued to give, I gave less and less but still took just as much as I'd been taking, getting without giving. I was selfish and inattentive, not realizing that you can't grow unless you give.[72]

As I took and took and took, the distance between us widened, and soon enough our Us Box was empty, depleted because I wasn't contributing—I wasn't focused on the relationship like I had been during all those magnificent days together, back when everything felt so effortless. Turns out that it takes immense effort to make something feel that effortless.

And so while the last few years have taught me that we are *not* the sum of our material possessions, I now know the obverse is also true: we *are* what we focus on.

Unfortunately, by the time I realized this, it was too late. Our strained relationship faltered for months after the fall, vacillating between all the sad and angry emotions of a love song, attempting to find the rhythm we'd lost, only to realize that our syncopated love had fallen out of a step and that neither of us could find the the beat again.

I'm reminded of an old Iraqi fable I once read in which a merchant in Baghdad sends his servant to the marketplace for provisions. Soon, the servant comes home white and trembling and tells the merchant that in the marketplace he was jostled by a woman, whom he recognized as Death, and she made a threatening gesture. Borrowing the merchant's horse, the servant flees at top speed to Samarra, where he believes Death will not find him. The merchant then goes to the marketplace and finds Death and asks why she made the threatening gesture. She replies, "That was not a threatening gesture; it was only a start of surprise. I was astonished to see him in Baghdad, for I had an appointment with him tonight in Samarra."

Somehow, I let the inverse happen to Colleen and me: I ran toward the place where I thought Happiness was, when Happiness was actually waiting in the place I was running from. I know this now, but only after the fall. Sometimes the best teacher is our most recent failure.

10 || Thoreau & the Unabomber Walk into a Bar

OCTOBER 2012

If there's a God, I imagine he lives in a cabin somewhere in Western Montana. I'd bet he doesn't frequent this bar, though. The air around me smells like a sad song: cigarette smoke and spilled beer and cheap perfume, the kind that never washes off. I'm not sure what I'm doing here; I don't even drink. Ryan dragged me here amid my verbal kicking and screaming.

"Are both you guys available?" Whatshername asks from behind the bar. Through her rural twang I can't tell whether it's a question or a statement.

"Available for what?"

"For *sex*. Are you boys available for sex?"

"Oh. Umm, yes," Ryan says with a billboard smile, "by invitation only, though."

Whatshername is cute, maybe twenty-five but looks every day of thirty-four, and has on too much makeup and a pushup bra for extra tips. Even in the dingy light she's blotchy with a hand-me-down face, and you can tell she's a heavy smoker. There's a butterfly tattoo at the small of her back; I can't read the inscription below its wings, but I think I understand what it really says. Ryan has been talking to this girl and her two friends for fifteen excruciating minutes. Both friends are seated on this side of the bar and are both slightly more serrated versions of the bartender, their lacquered faces dry and cracking from the lack of humidity. I haven't said much up to this point, but I'm exhausted just spectating this tete-a-tete.

Ryan glances over and smirks in my direction and then pulls a sip of liquid the color of urine from a shotglass. They pour drinks in this town like they're trying to get rid of overstock. A couple bucks could get you shitfaced here, a fact that strikes me as unbearably sad. The tip jar on the counter is half empty. A song is playing on the jukebox. Literally, a *jukebox*. I recognize the melody as Austin Harley-Leonard's "Ohio," which makes me feel like the gods pre-planned this irony since the song is about finding a way back to Ohio and then never leaving again, a tempting thought that makes me pat my pocket to check for car keys.

Studies suggest that surgeons who listen to music during operations perform better than the ones who don't. Trains of thoughts rush through my head, random facts like this one race from one side to the other, especially when I'm faced with uninteresting situations like this. Sometimes I wish I could turn it off. The thoughts come and go; I'm never able to hold onto them. Besides, if I held onto them they'd be mine to keep and I'd be responsible for them, and frankly that's entirely too much to commit to.

"To availability!" Ryan proclaims and raises his snifter of piss.[73] (Like me, Ryan is also recently single.)

All three girls giggle in a strange multi-tonal unison that seems mimetic of farm animals mating. Ryan looks in my direction and, based on his reaction to my expression, my look staring back at him must betray confusion or terror or excitement or somehow all three at the same time. I'm not sure which; I was just trying to smile politely.

Smiling helps boost the immune system.

Earlier this year, before the Ohio humidity was thick enough to taste, Ryan and I embarked on our first-ever book tour, a thirty-three-city endeavor, to support the publication our first full-length nonfiction book, *Minimalism: Live a Meaningful Life*, which uses the concepts of minimalism to outline and discuss the five most important areas of life: health, relationships, passion, growth, and contribution. That tour, which ended in mid-July, lugged us all over the US and Canada, and its episodes helped birth a new Joshua and Ryan. An inexchangable experience. Suffice it to say, we have learned more—experienced more—than we expected. Below are some selections from my journal, a random, frame-by-frame collage of our travels this year....

We have had our car towed in St. Petersburg, Florida. We have now worked from the same beach where I scattered my mother's ashes two years prior. We have hugged Occupiers and attorneys and Couch Surfers and retired-CEOs. We have met a Knoxville man who fasted for forty days.

We have been pulled over and searched for drugs by the Kansas state highway patrol.[74] We have slept on a kind couples' floor in Missouri and listened as their Tourettic neighbor howled obscenities throughout the night. We have slept in our car in the middle of the Arizona desert a few feet from poisonous insects and snakes. We have (well, I have) vomited in a San Francisco bathroom minutes before speaking to our largest crowd of the tour.[75] We have drunk the best tea in the world with our new friend Leo Babauta. We have, from a distance, mistaken the bright lights of Reno for the bright lights of Vegas. We have been stranded in a blizzard in rural Wyoming. We have searched (unsuccessfully) for John Stockton's bronze statue in Salt Lake City. We have slept in a stunning warehouse-district loft in Milwaukee. We have awkwardly signed autographs in Chicago on New Year's Eve-eve. We have had meaningful conversations with an eighty-three-year-old woman and an eleven-year-old boy.

We have showered with Texas well water. We have spent time with Colin Wright when our paths crossed as he zig-zagged the US. We have walked in the rain with our author friend Chase Night and two beautiful red-headed twins in Little Rock. We have appeared on NPR in St. Louis with the legendary Don Marsh. We have exercised at rest stops in dozens of states. We have been recognized by readers on the streets of Nashville and Dayton and, later, in Seattle.[76] We have thanked people like John Schultz for driving up to eight hours to meet us in Arkansas and Oklahoma and Kansas.

We have eaten fish tacos in Rochester. We have smashed a writing hand—my right hand—in a faulty window and bled all over Coney Island. We have read aloud a three-page sentence from my forthcoming novel in front of a modest-sized crowd in NYC. We have fallen *up* the stairs while exiting the subway in Manhattan. We have witnessed a white Scottish terrier wearing an argyle sweater smoking a Camel Light in Brooklyn.[77] We have taken our message to the streets of Boston—literally. We have fed homeless people on the streets of Pittsburgh and read poems from our friend Shawn Mihalik's poetry collection in Cleveland. We have graded homework for my new online writing class, How to Write Better, while driving east on I-70. We have given an MLK-style speech at the steps of the Lincoln Memorial. We have seen "the largest condom store" (in the world?) in Philadelphia.

We have stood next to a giant, surreal Ronald Reagan head in Branson, Missouri. We have spoken in bookstores and cultural centers and university classrooms. We have taken turns passenger-seat sleeping while on the road. We have started a fake band just for the hell of it.[78] We have told lame jokes in front of a standing-room-only crowd at NYC's Housing Works, from which 100% of the event's proceeds went toward fighting the dual crises of homelessness and AIDS. We have autographed (defaced?) books and wallets and even a few Kindles. We have walked in the rain, navigated subways, and ridden countless trains. We have unabashedly groomed each other and discovered that we both use the same hair product.[79] We have witnessed some unbelievably ignorant bumperstickers.[80] We have stayed with amazing new friends like Donna and Emily and Sarah and long-time friends like Dave and Jeff and Marla.

We have driven from Ohio to Des Moines and Portland and San Diego, where our bright-eyed friend Austen introduced us to a hole-in-the-wall Mexican restaurant that was still open at 1 a.m. We have shoveled horse poop in front of a polygamist family while the sun receded into Utah's mountains. We have visited Mount Rushmore and had much of the experience tainted by myriad advertisements and entire towns predicated on buying shit. We have driven past grass greener than AstroTurf in high-def, so green that we weren't sure if we were in North Dakota or Ireland. We have witnessed Independence Day fireworks in downtown Boise. We have parked on the side of the road to take in the ferocious forest fires of Colorado, bright and blood-orange and uncontrollable as they lit up the night sky. We have spoken alongside our new friend Joshua Becker at the World Domination Summit. We have slept in a supposedly sleepless Seattle. We have watched the sun set cinematically over the water during our final meetup in Vancouver. We have spent time in Canada, staying up late and laughing with Leslie and Julia and company, playing guitar and singing songs, spending quality time with some of the most amazing people we've ever met.

We have seen both coasts. We have driven more than twenty thousand miles in our tour bus.[81] We have set foot in forty-four US states. We have traveled more during our thirty-first year on earth than the previous thirty combined. We have enjoyed thirty-three outstanding meetups in thirty-three unique cities. We have spoken in front of more than a thousand people this year, with audiences ranging from two to seventy-two people. We have laughed and cried and laughed at the fact we were crying. We have eaten meals and had meaningful conversations with wonderful people doing wonderful things, all of whom we first met on the Internet. We have made new friends. We have been inspired by scores of people and their amazing stories of transformation. We have, in our own small little way, helped spread the message of simple living. We have lived life, and we have never felt more alive. We have stopped talking about living and started living.

End flash-cut collage.

After the curtain had closed on the tour in Vancouver, we were elated but exhausted, ready to embrace Ohio again with open arms, even with its muggy air and barrage of windshield insects. We began our trek back to the Buckeye State, and along the way we bore witness to what is perhaps the most visually astonishing place on earth: Western Montana, driving past its flannel plains and evergreen mountains and skylines from a cowboy cliche, and past its cobalt rivers overhung with century-old pines with flecklets of sunlight through them on the water bending downriver, to the place beyond its sprawling canyons, where fields divided by train cars simmer in the summer heat and time stands still.

It would sound cliche to say we immediately knew that she was the one. But at first sight, we immediately knew that she was the one. Montana, with her three hundred fifty days of sunshine,[82] rightfully christened the Last Best Place, was the place we wanted to begin working on our next big thing. We knew that if we wanted to continue to spread our simple-living message, then the time had come for us to hunker down and do some serious work, what musicians sometimes refer to as *woodshedding*. And we knew that to get what we want, we must be willing to take action; we must be willing to do the work.

On that account, Ryan and I moved into a mountainside cabin in Western Montana. As of October 2012, we are residents of the Treasure State, two Ohio transplants residing in a remote area, two hours from the Idaho panhandle, one hour outside Butte, just in time for its notorious subarctic climate, sort of doing an updated version of the whole Thoreau thing.[83][84]

These days, I have little desire for new material possessions (although that baleful yearning still lingers from time to time), but I do want to be successful. And success for me has little to do with money or possessions or status. Rather, success is a simple equation: Happiness + Growth + Contribution = Success. That's the only kind of success I know. Hence, I want to partake in work that makes me happy, work that encourages me to grow, work that helps me contribute beyond myself. Ultimately, I want to create more and consume less. Doing so requires real work.

Within the walls of our new home, before the sun sets on 2012, I'm going to finally publish my novel, *As a Decade Fades*, after nearly four years of bleeding onto the page. Plus, Ryan and I are planning a ten-city Holiday Tour, as well as beginning work on our next book: a currently untitled narrative nonfiction project, a memoirish sort of book.[85]

It's every author's cliched dream—to find a mountainside cabin with picturesque views, to toss another log on the crackling winter fire as snow blankets the ice-covered river beyond the windowpanes, to remove the distractions of the emotionally exhaustive rat race and start working on his or her most important work—right?

Alright, maybe that's not everyone's aspiration, but the time seemed right for us to do just that: to relocate to a secluded spot in Big Sky Country to work vigorously, learn ferociously, and grow immensely.

Consequently, for at least the next four months—perhaps longer—we're going to hole up in our new home in the wilderness and focus.[86]

When I first arrived on October 3, after a two thousand-mile trek from Dayton, I was greeted by an early snowfall that robbed autumn of her color. I knew straightaway that a productive winter was around the bend. While taking in the scenery, I chopped wood to prepare for the forthcoming winter months. Ryan tootled into town a week later and together we colonized our new livingspace.

The cabin itself is situated on the side of a mountain, on the outskirts of this five-bar, five-church town. There's one traffic light within thirty-seven-hundred square miles of this place. After a few days of early October snow, the accumulation ceased, and autumn fell back again after the blanket of white faded. This time of year here is azure blue and forest green and a thousand shades of yellow. Even the bark on the trees is a brownish yellow, leaving everything looking comfortably burnt.

And yet with all my chatter about staying focused and being productive, here I am now in a two-bit bar listening to some banjo song pollute the soundwaves around me.

This too shall pass.

It's dark outside now, and through opaque windows I can see that our car is the only non-4-wheel-drive vehicle parked on the street. Both girls on this side of the bar are sporting dull, gold wedding bands with tiny diamonds, although that doesn't keep them from flirting heavily. I look down and catch my thumb playing with the empty skin near the knuckle of the fourth finger on my lefthand. It's been three years since that ring slipped off and I still feel a pang of guilt, doubly so because of my recent break-up with Colleen; it's either a congenital guilt or that ceaseless milieu of shame that lingers from too many Catholic masses as a child. My hands are rough, my Rustbelt-summertime tan has faded, and my skin is now the color of wet thermal underwear.

The girl next to me is paying me too much attention. I've hardly said a word, but she says she finds me "interesting," which is a term I would use passive-aggressively, a back-handed insult, but I can tell that she really means it. I'm *interesting*. Good for me. She's coughing now, a phlegmy smoker's cough. Her breath is overdressed in cheap red wine.

There is more alcohol in mouthwash than in wine.

I never realized it until this moment, but a *cough* is onomatopoeic. These two girls, swarthy and orangeishly faux tan, could pass as sisters, though they're clearly not. They look too similar to be siblings, as if they're actually trying to look like they're related. I'm certain they've told me their names sometime in the last fifteen minutes, but I haven't been able to focus, so I imagine they're both named Betty.

The fear of ugly people is called cacophobia.

The bar is smoky; the smoke just sort of hangs in the air. You're not allowed to smoke indoors in this state, but this middle-of-nowhere bar doesn't even bother with the obligatory signage. You could earn a bachelor's degree in apathy just from sitting in this place for an evening. My ass aches from the barstool's cold hardness.

The bathroom here is plausible only in a horror film. Once white, the urinal dividers are now a deep rust-brown from years of bad aim and splatter. The sink is a badly stained stainless-steel trough. The electric hand dryer dangles from the wall, inoperable, its exposed wires just inches from running water.

Twenty minutes ago, I returned from the bathroom to find my barstool seized by six feet of camouflage. Ryan was sitting on his same stool (the one he's still perched on now, right here next to me), while a skinny man in flea-market army fatigues attempted to sell him "freesh keeled" deer meat at a substantial discount, which meat the man referred to as "vinsin." Have you ever noticed that when we eat mammals we never claim to eat the actual animal itself? We don't eat deer meat; we eat venison. We don't eat cow sandwiches; we eat hamburgers. We don't devour pig flesh; we enjoy Jimmy Dean breakfast sausages. So forth and so on. Is this because we feel guilty? Do hunters feel some sort of strange guilt after killing for sport? Is hunting an actual sport, like say basketball or baseball? It suddenly occurs to me that the complete sum of what I know about hunting could be inscribed on a .22 caliber shell casing in size-twenty font.

The hunter sat there on my stool and negotiated with Ryan. He talked loudly, methamphetaminicly, and Ryan just sat there and politely tolerated his manic sales pitch. The hunter looked ridiculous, like a parody of himself, with his one-size-too-big fatigues and almost comic-like concave features—his dark, sunken, colorless eyes with bags the color of internal hemorrhaging under them; his large nose outlined by shadowy crevices; his weak chin covered by a week and a half of spotty stubble, which was negligent in its apparent duty to cover the crater-like pockmarks mantling this man's cheeks—and there was a half-smoked cigarette tucked behind his left ear. His hair was receding badly but was long in the back. And his boots had flecklets of blood on them. Was it deer blood? There was really no way to tell.

Peladophobia is the fear of bald people.

I sat down next to them and pretended to sip a diet cola that tasted eerily like creekwater (*eerily* because there's a creek almost directly behind this fine establishment). I imagined Ryan stopping the hunter midsentence and asking, "Where do you get your hair cut?"

"What?" I imagined the confused hunter would respond.

"Your haircut. Where do you go to get it done?"

"Huh?"

"I just want to know so I can avoid that barbershop at all costs." But Ryan would never say this, so he didn't. He didn't buy any freesh-keeled vinsin either.

Thirty minutes go by, though it feels like a week. Time falls from the clock slower here.

"If you write about this, please don't make this town sound like it's just a bunch of drunks," Ryan warns me.

"Which town?" I say.

"*This* town. P———."

"But it *is* filled with a bunch of drunks. It's a drinking town with a fishing problem."

"What?"

"That's what that ridiculous bumpersticker on one of the

pickups outside says: *P——, MT, a small drinkin' town with a big fishin' problem.*"

"Whatever. Just don't write about it."

"OK I won't," I fib.

Ryan furrows his brow.

"What? I won't mention the *name* of the town. It's not like I'd write 'P—— is filled with a bunch of drunks' or anything."

"I'm serious."

"But look at this place," I hold my arms out not unlike I'm being crucified.

"What about it?"

"I imagine hell is a smalltown bar like this. Or at least purgatory. Like, you know, you have to wait it out. Survive this, and God will make His judgment," I say, my arms still nailed to the smoky air.

In ancient Rome, crucifixion was usually intended to provide a death that was particularly slow, publicly humiliating, and painful (hence the term excruciating, which literally means 'out of crucifying').

It's not like the people in this town are dumb or ignorant. They aren't. In fact, if anyone's ignorant in this context, it's me. I've never been "huntin'." I haven't touched a fishing pole since adolescence. And I've never owned a pick-up truck or a gunrack or camouflage anything. No, these people aren't ignorant at all; they've simply adapted to their environment. New people don't come around here often, and when they do, the people in this town are slow to react, curious spectators waiting for something exciting to happen.

"What are you boys doing tonight?" Whatshername asks from the other side of the bar, and then looks at the Bettys to see whether they're listening.

I just look at her but don't respond. Among the increasing

chatter and the errant background music, everyone in here sounds vaguely payphoneish when they speak.

"I'm out of your league," I imagine Ryan responding to the bartender, though that's not something he'd ever say either.

"You boys want to smoke some pot after this?" one of the Bettys asks the air around Ryan and me.

Ryan cocks his head and looks at her puzzled. It's getting louder in here as more people arrive, and I feel the queer urge to shout something loud and obscene toward the mounting crowd, toward no one in particular, but I'm not sure why.

"What, you boys aren't cops, are you?" the other Betty asks. Her eyes are the color of a lighter's small flame.

People with blue eyes are better able to see in the dark. Blue eyes are actually an evolutionary mutation. Before the mutation occurred, all humans had brown eyes.

Ryan does in fact look like a cop, not a real-life police officer, more like a TV cop: handsome with a jutting jawline, broad-shouldered, a five o'clock shadow.

A man's beard grows faster when he is anticipating sex.

And the aviator sunglasses tucked into Ryan's shirt collar don't exactly scream "I'm not a cop!"

The other Betty holds her wedding-ringed hand to her mouth and hacks up a deep cough, which prompts this Betty to cough too.

This place is flooded with flannel and haphazard cleavage. Whatshername informs us that the bar isn't ever this crowded on a weeknight. "They all came in to see you two," she says. "To size you up."

"To size us up?" I ask, faking concern.

"Yes, honey. They all just want to get a whiff of the new guys," she says while motioning toward the pack of feral dogs congregated on bar stools and around pool tables, all steeping in bar smoke. "Heard a lot about you boys. 'Snot everyday that a couple writers move into town. Especially two as good lookin' as y'all. They think it's like something out of the movies."

I just blink in response. Locals are all around us now, swarming. They've stormed this bar like the beaches of Normandy.

"The girls in this town are a horny bunch," she ensures us, although I'm not quite sure why. A warning? An offering? "And they like you Hollywood types."

Celebriphilia is the abnormally intense desire to have sex with a celebrity.

I've never even been to Hollywood. I look down at my feet and then around at the neon oozing from the walls, and I feel a strong urge to find an exit. I'm not sure whether it's agoraphobia or claustrophobia or what, but there are too many people here and I don't feel comfortable. I might be many things, but I'm not alone. But then again, loneliness and aloneness are not the same thing: a crowded room can be the loneliest place on the planet.

I tell Ryan that I'm headed outside in search of fresh air, and I find the strength to deliver my body through the tavern doors. Outside, a truck backs into the street; its exhaust is authoritative and obnoxious and it spits flint-colored hockey-stick-shaped fumes into the air. Its bumpersticker says MONTUCKY. As it backs out, its headlights illuminate an unaccompanied girl standing at the bar's exterior.

The opposite of reverse is actually obverse.

The girl takes a drag from a cigarette and looks over at me suspiciously. She's less than ten feet away and in the pale light she looks a lot like a young Jennifer Aniston.

Celebriphilia is the abnormally intense desire to have sex with a celebrity.

It's cold outside and I realize my coat's too thin. Astronomically, the Big Sky here is usually clear and lovely. Not tonight though. Tonight, layers of rhino-colored clouds billow low in the atmosphere, touching the ranges on either side of me as if they're bolted to pitons in the mountainside. The smoking girl looks tentative, nervous even. She's wearing a big coat but is still shivering. Covering her own mouth with a gloved hand, she sneezes and then wipes her nose on the back of the glove.

The technical term for sneezing is sternutation.

"You're not going to try to bum a cigarette from me, are you?" is the first thing she asks me, looking at me with scaring eyes.

Fruit flies have been known to drink alcohol after being rejected by a potential mate.

"I don't smoke," I reply. "But now I'm tempted to ask for one."

She winces. "I'm sorry. That was a real bitchy thing to say. It's just that I'm trying to quit, and this is supposed to be my last pack." She is staring at her cigarette's glowing tip like a lit fuse.

I step closer, just outside her personal space, and she stops shivering as much. She has a manic, deer-in-headlights look about her. From this distance I notice how much I tower over this girl.

A person who is six-two is taller than ninety-four percent of the world's population.

She offers me a cigarette, a sort of apologetic truce, with a smile I'd like to take home and keep. I wave it off with a hand and inch closer. She's short and pretty, and by her manner she seems terrified of something—of me or this town, of the thought of giving up her bad habit, the thought of committing to something for the rest of her life. Whatever it is, it terrifies her. I'm so close that I can see myself in her gray eyes. For a moment I imagine her going back to my place, smelling like smoke and spilled beer and cheap perfume, crawling into my bed, and staining my sheets with an hour's worth of faked love and then falling asleep to the pulse of tainted excitement. I could spend the next hour or two trying to talk to this girl. I could try to find some common ground that doesn't exist. But I don't have it in me tonight. I'm thirty-one now, and I've untangled myself from my lotus-eating twenties, and so sex for sex's sake seems like a vacant proposition, devoid of meaning. Lonely.

Vasocongestion is the medical term for blueballs.... The word masturbation comes from the Latin word masturbari, which means "to pollute oneself."

I look back at the bar's entrance and decide not to say goodbye to anyone. I'd rather just go home alone, which somehow feels less lonely than the alternative. Behind the brick buildings, the creek rakes the rocks and the sediment. I realize I have to piss. I nod down at the pretty girl and tell her to have a good night and to be safe, and she returns to her cigarette, shivering, without hesitation, and I start the trek back home, in search of a place to urinate along the way.

Every year, roughly forty thousand Americans suffer from toilet-related injuries. By peeing in the shower, however, the average American can save one thousand one hundred and fifty-seven gallons of water per annum.[87]

Back at the cabin, two flies swarm around my upstairs bedroom, searching for an exit. Both creatures are massive and unhurried and fairly obtuse, annoying but easy to kill. It's dark and my bed is empty. But tomorrow the work begins.

11 || Beautiful Accidents

DECEMBER 2012

As we drive up to Toronto's Centre for Social Innovation, I'm certain we've arrived at the wrong place. After double checking the address, I grow worried that whoever is here to attend our little meetup won't be able to make it past the line of people outside.

TCSI is a large brick building with five stories of meeting areas, conference rooms, and shared workspace. Mel,[88] the wonderful Torontonian who found us this venue for our little meetup, doesn't answer her phone. Her voicemail picks up instead.

"Hey, it's Joshua," I say, my worry beginning to turn into panic, which I can hear in my own voice. "There's a line in front of our building. Looks like there's another event going on tonight—a concert or a party or something. Call me back when you get a moment, and let me know whether there's a way to get our attendees around the crowd out front—a back entrance, secret trapdoor, a fire escape, something. Thanks, bye."

This month marks exactly two years since Ryan and I started our website. We are roughly halfway through our ten-city Holiday

Tour, having just left Boston a few days ago where we spoke to modest-sized group at Harvard Business School. There's nowhere to park outside TCSI, and the adjacent lot is full, so we park in a "reserved parking" spot that doesn't say who it's reserved for, though one thing's for certain: it's not reserved for us.

Ryan and I walk past the crowd, up to the main entrance, a glass double door that leads to an elevator and a stairwell. A sign taped to the window says, "The Minimalists' Holiday Happiness Tour, Fifth Floor, 7 p.m." There isn't a sign to indicate what other, larger event is happening concurrent to ours.

The line that's bulging out the door resembles a crowd waiting to see a concert and is snaked up the stairwell. As we make our way up each flight, apologizing—excuse me, pardon me, excuse me—every few steps, we keep getting shy waves and twinkly smiles and surprised looks from almost every person we pass. It becomes increasingly apparent that at least some of these smiling faces are here to see us. It's impossible to determine what percentage though.

A cute brunette is standing at the top of the stairs on the fifth floor, directing traffic. It's Mel. She looks overwhelmed.

"Hey, I tried to call you," I say, extending my arms for a hug.

"Sorry, I left my phone in the room," she throws a thumb over her shoulder, and then gives us both a hug.

"What are all these people here for?" Ryan asks.

She looks at him contemplatively, unsure whether he's joking, and then, when she can tell that he's not, she looks at us both incredulously, donning an expression that says, *They're all here for you, you dipshits.*

Ryan looks at me. I look at him. Realization breaks across our features at precisely the same moment. "Oh shit," we say in unison. The line is coiled down the five flights of stairs behind us.

"We should let some of these people in the room," I say, attempting to help somehow.

"The room is already full," she says. "I thought you said there would be like forty or fifty people, max."

Down the hall, our meeting space is white and bright and brimming with Canadians—men and women and children, all ages, all races, all…waiting for us? The high-ceilinged room likely holds fifty people comfortably, but there's more like a hundred people inside, shoulder to shoulder, wall to wall, pushed all the way to the back. Mel's friend Erika, a tall brunette in jeans with her hair pulled back, ushers us toward the front of the room, casting a Moses-like vibe that forces the dense crowd to part down the middle, forming an opening that leads to the stage. Ryan and I stare blankly at the mass of bodies in front of us. It's ten minutes till seven.

It turns out that three of Canada's largest newspapers all decided to run full-page coverage leading up to our event this week. Thankfully, a few minutes before Ryan and I took the stage, Mel commandeered a large meeting hall in the building's concrete basement. Even then with the considerably larger space, we are forced to present our disquisition twice to accommodate the number of people here.

It's almost nine o'clock now, and we're getting ready to do our whole impromptuish speech all over again. The large room we're in is crammed with rows of chairs leading up to a slightly elevated stage. There's a short dividing wall to my left, separating us from the TCSI's in-house coffee shop, overtop of which you can hear the muted sounds of milk being steamed and the dings of an old-fashioned cash register. The lights focused on the stage make the crowd kind of hard to see. Even so, I notice my friend Aili sitting in the front row, stage right.

Aili is a former student of the online writing class I began teaching earlier this year. She looks especially Scandinavian-looking in this light—tall and blonde and pretty. Her eyes are the color of well-worn jeans with the same bottomless quality of a vast ocean. She is dressed casually but in a sort of well-thought-out kind of way. Premeditated casual, I guess you could call it. Her accent is clearly Canadian, proper and confident and breathy. If you talk to her for more than thirty seconds, it's easy to see that she's smarter than you. At least this is true in my case. Although, to be fair, Aili's story is not unlike mine: In her late twenties, she had the world by the balls. Well, at least ostensibly.[89] After graduating from a distinguished university, she found herself in a well-paying job, working her way up the ranks, accumulating all the trappings of the American Dream along the way.[90] She was living the life she was supposed to want, but it wasn't *her* life; she felt like she was living someone else's dream.

Ryan and I had a free day in Toronto yesterday, so Aili and I met for tea at a coffee shop called Darkhorse, while Ryan spent some time at our PR agent's office on King Street.[91] Aili and I sat at a table near the window, and everything about our conversation seemed to vibrate on the same frequency as we ruminated over life changes, living more simply, and, most memorably, balance.

"Balance in life is hard to find," she said, an acoustic song playing quietly through the ceiling's speakers. I recognized the song as "Unwriteable Girl" by Gregory Alan Isakov, whose gentle voice seemed to stir the melody into the air around us.

"Depends on what you mean by balance, no?"

"Exactly. It's difficult to even define, nebulous. The concept itself is enough to make you feel like you're not enough in every aspect of life, especially if you're driven to achieve; at home and at work, you feel like you should be doing more—contributing more, getting more stuff done, being more available. More, more, more. Where's the balance in that? All the silly SMART goals and aggressive schedules supported by a tidal wave of strategies and tools, all in one big attempt to steer the ship in a new direction as the question still lingers."

"The question being, How can I find balance?"

"Yes. Which makes me wonder whether it's even the right question," Aili continues. "Here's the thing about balance: it creates separation between work and the rest of your life. But work isn't separate from life, it's part of it. So rather than trying to measure and weigh and compare parts of your life that defy comparison, why not ask yourself whether you're feeling the harmony in how it all adds up. Like, am I happy? Am I healthy? Is what I'm doing meaningful to me? Do I love my life?"

"Those questions are highly individual, though."

"I think they have to be," she said. "Only *you* can figure out what makes *you* happy. It's not a template."

"I agree," I said, earnestly. "I used to think of *work* as a bad word. Back in the corporate world, work was something that prevented me from living, something that kept me from feeling satisfied or fulfilled or passionate. Even the word itself carried with it a negative connotation. Work—*bluck!* When I left the corporate world, I swore off the word altogether. Noun, verb, adjective—I avoided all of work's iterations. I no longer 'went to work,' so that was easy to remove from my vocabulary. In fact, I no longer 'worked' at all; instead I replaced the word with a more specific verb: I would 'write' or 'teach' or 'speak' or 'volunteer,' but I refused to 'work.' I no longer went to the gym to 'workout'; instead I 'exercised.' And I stopped wearing 'work clothes'; I chose instead to wear 'dress clothes.' And I avoided getting 'worked up,' preferring to call it 'stress' or 'anxiety.' And I didn't bring my car to the shop to get 'worked on,' deciding instead to have my vehicle 'repaired.' Hell, I even avoided 'handiwork' [92] and 'housework,' selecting their more banal alternatives. Suffice it to say, I wanted nothing to do with the word. I wanted it not only stricken from my lexicon, but from my memory, erasing every shred of the thing that kept me from pursuing my dream for over a decade. But after a year of that nonsense, I realized something: it wasn't the word that was bad; it was the meaning I gave to the word. It took removing the word from my everyday speech for a year to discover that it wasn't a bad word at all. During that year, I *had* been pursuing my dream, and guess what—when I looked over my shoulder at everything I'd accomplished, I realized that pursuing my dream was, in fact, a lot of work. It took a lot of work to grow a website. It took a lot of work to publish five books. It took a lot of work to embark on a coast-to-coast tour. It took a lot of work to teach my first writing class. It took a lot of work to pursue my dream. Work wasn't the problem. What I did as my work was the problem. I wasn't passionate about my work before—my work wasn't my mission—and so I wanted to escape from work so I could live a more rewarding life, looking to balance out the tedium of the daily grind. But work and life don't work that way. Even when you're pursuing your dream, there will be times of boredom and stress and long stretches of drudgery. That's alright. It's all worth it in the end. When your work becomes your life's mission, you no longer need a work-life balance."

"You obviously weren't satisfied with your corporate life," Aili said.

"Nope. Far from satisfied. I'm sure you struggled with balance in your corporate days too, right?"

"Yes, I knew something needed to change, but I had no idea what it was."

"What did you do to figure it out?" I asked.

"I'm sure it seemed crazy to the people around me—it even seemed a little crazy to me—but I knew the only way to figure it out was to re-evaluate everything, even those things that were so deeply ingrained in my life that it felt like they were part of me."

"Like what?" I asked.

"Like my nine-year relationship with the same guy. Like my own home. My salary with benefits. My rising career. My concept of success. My assumptions about what my life was supposed to be. All of it."

"That's hard to do," I said.

"It was. But with everything in question, it was almost like I finally saw the light: I was never going to feel happy or complete based on anything outside of me. It needed to come from me—from inside me."

"A heavy realization. What'd you do then?"

"One by one, I let everything go," she said, "and underneath it all I uncovered something unexpected."

"What did you find?"

"I found myself—the real *me*. Self-acceptance. Connection. Empowerment. The joy and excitement of the here and now," she said with joy livening her pretty face. Her smile could sell things.

Four hours of conversation like this, and now she's seated in the front row while I'm on stage, which makes me a little nervous.

This writing-on-the-Internet stuff is a little like magic. Never did I imagine I could meet and connect with so many amazing people, so many like-minded folks with similar interests and values and beliefs. But here I am, here we are, in front of a standing-room-only crowd. It's a little surreal.

Ryan looks over and nudges me after seeing the awe on my face. He leans over and in a soft whisper reminds me that these people aren't here to see *us*; they're here for the message. Our theme for this tour revolves around the holidays, which for many people is the most stressful time of the year. People are looking for answers and new ways to look at our consumer-driven culture. I nod and say thank you. Ryan has a way of keeping me in line, humble, grounded.

The room is full, a bit cramped, the crowd filling their seats. It's snowing lightly through the half-windows behind the stage, just a few flurries coating the sidewalks above this basement. The windows weep from the indoor heat. I turn on the microphone and look over the crowd, avoiding eye contact, which'd just make me more nervous than I already am. I tend to get almost cataleptic in front of a microphone, and it takes a good two minutes before the room fades away—the way it does in movies—and I get my rhythm, and then when I get going it's almost like I have an off-brand type of gustatory synesthesia, where I can almost taste the words before they exit my mouth, and then everything is just fine.

I begin my spiel by telling a story about a child on Christmas morning: "Fast forward a few weeks from now, Christmas Day, as little Andrew unwraps Optimus Prime and a grin breaks across his features when the large toy lights up and nearly comes to life, flashing and beeping and driving Andy's parents crazy.

"But in a few moments, Andy discards the toy and begins unwrapping the rest of his presents, extracting each box from under the tree, one by one—some long, some tall, some heavy, some light. Each box reveals a new toy. Each shred of green-and-red wrapping paper, a flash of happiness.

"An hour later, though, little Andy is crying hysterically. Based on his fits, this has undoubtedly been the worst Christmas ever.

Sure, Andrew received many of the things on his list, but he's far more concerned with what he didn't receive. That Power Ranger he wanted, that video game system he was secretly hoping for, that new computer that all his friends are getting. The toys in front of him simply remind him of what he doesn't have.

"This sounds childish, I know, but don't we do the same thing? Don't we often look at the things around us and wish we had more? Don't we covet that new car, those new clothes, that new iPhone?"

Several people in the crowding are nodding with identification.

"What if Andy was happy with the toys in front of him? And what if we were too?" I ask rhetorically.

After a brief pause, Ryan jumps in: "We are clearly in the throes of the holiday shopping season," he says, speaking through his handheld microphone.

"Take a look around. Malls are packed with herds of consumers. Storefronts are decorated in green and red. The jingly commercials are running nonstop. The holiday season has officially peeked its gigantic, mass-mediated noggin around the corner. It's here, and if we rely solely on billboards and store signage, then we might believe we have to participate.

"Retailers prepare months in advance for this—preparation that's meant to stimulate your insatiable desire to consume: Doorbuster sales. New products. Gigantic two-page ads. TV, radio, print, billboards. Sale, sale, sale! Early bird specials. One day only! Get the best deal. Act now! While supplies last.

"Joshua and I would, however, like to shed some light on this shopping—*ahem*, holiday—season. Each year around this time, we all feel that warm-'n'-fuzzy Christmastime nostalgia associated with the onset of winter. We break out the scarves and the gloves and the winter coats. We go ice-skating and sledding and eat hearty meals with our extended families. We take days off from work and spend time with our loved ones and give thanks for the gift of life.

"The problem is that we've been conditioned to associate this joyous time of year—the mittens and decorations and the family activities—with purchasing material items. We've trained ourselves to believe that buying stuff is an inextricable part of Christmas. We all know, however, that the holidays needn't require gifts to be meaningful. Rather, this time of year is meaningful because of its true meaning—not the wrapped boxes we place under the tree. I'm not saying that there's anything inherently wrong or bad about gift-giving during this time of year. However, when purchasing gifts becomes the focal point of the season, we lose focus on what's truly important.

"Instead of concentrating on holiday shopping," Ryan continues, "I'd like to encourage you to take five steps toward a more meaningful Christmas together:

"Step one. Avoid holiday doorbuster sales. Whether it's Black Friday or any of the subsequent big shopping weekends, it's best to stay inside. It's important to understand that consumption is an unquenchable thirst. Retailers and advertisers and manufacturers know this too well, and these sales are designed to take advantage of our insatiable desire to consume. Instead, support your local businesses; support the people in your community who are making a difference.

"Step two. Gift your time. If you could receive only one Christmas present this year, what would it be? The answer for me is simple: time. The best present is presence. You see, the people I care about mean much more to me than a new pair of shoes or a shiny new gadget or even a certified pre-owned luxury car with a huge bow on top. And yet, many of us attempt to give material items to make up for the time we don't spend with the people we love. I know—I did it for years. But possessions can't ever make up for lost time. The next time someone asks you what you want for Christmas, consider responding with, 'Your presence is the best present you can give me.'

"Step three. Gift experiences, not stuff. Here's an idea. What if you decided to gift only experiences this year? How much more memorable would your holidays be? Your experiences build and strengthen the bond between you and the people you care about. Some experiences worth gifting might include tickets to a concert or play, a home-cooked meal, breakfast in bed, a foot rub, a vacation together, watching a wintertime sunset sink into the horizon. Don't you think you'd find more value in these experiences than in material gifts? Don't you think your loved ones will find more value too?

"Step four. Ask for better Christmas gifts. I'd be remiss if I didn't discuss the gift of giving: the gift of contribution. You see, the age-old apothegm ends up being true: 'tis better to give than to receive. A few months ago, I gave my birthday to Charity Water and raised more than five thousand dollars from friends and family to gift clean water to more than two hundred and fifty people who didn't previously have access to it. Perhaps you can do the same this Christmas. Instead of gifts, you can ask people to donate to your favorite charity in your name. Wouldn't that feel better than a new necktie, pair of shoes, or piece of jewelry?

"Step five. We call this step Soup-Kitchen Christmas. You can do what we're doing this year and donate your time to a local soup kitchen or homeless shelter or foodbank or any place that needs volunteers. This year, Joshua and I will be in Vancouver during Christmas, where we and a local group of our readers will donate part of our Christmas Day to a soup kitchen who'll be able to really use our help during the holidays. You see, sometimes we have to contribute to help other people, but sometimes we need to contribute to help ourselves. When we step into our discomfort zones and contribute beyond ourselves, we grow, we experience the world in a different way, and we gain new perspectives from which to be thankful."

Ryan pauses for a moment to let it all sink in. Two-thirds of the crowd is nodding with vigor, the other third looks skeptical. Ryan blinks hard from the stage lights and continues, "If this all sounds a little preachy, I'm sorry. I am not here to preach to you. I'm not saying that you *have* to do, or that you *should* do, anything. The truth is that I know many of you are just like me. You're unhappy with the status quo, unhappy with what you're *supposed* to do with your life, just unhappy with the way things are. And so was I. But that's because I wasn't asking the right questions. ..." Ryan keeps talking. We banter back and forth on the stage for half an hour, telling the crowd about our back story and how we discovered minimalism and Ryan's Packing Party, followed by an hour of Q&A and then a book-signing and photographs, and eventually it's nearing midnight and the room is cleared out.

This entire journey seems like one giant beautiful accident. As Ryan and I exit the building, exhausted but also hopped-up on adrenaline, I spot Aili and her friend Julie waiting outside the main entrance. The winter air is cruel and crisp, wielding a sting that reminds me how alive I am. The four of us exchange hugs and Aili asks us what we're doing, says there's a nice restaurant down the street that's open late, would we like to go there with them, have a latenight meal, drinks, a conversation? Yes, yes we would.[93]

At some point during our meal, Aili asks me whether I still own a suit.

"Only my birthday suit," I respond.

"Really, you got rid of *all* your suits?"

"After wearing them six days a week for many years, I decided I didn't want to anymore—ever. So I don't."

"I ask because I've been thinking about doing some wardrobe reevaluation myself."

"Oh?"

"Yes, I hate my dress pants. They don't feel like *me*. And yet I hold on to them because they fit and are supposedly *nice*."

"I make it a rule to own only clothes I love to wear," I say.

"I like that. I've recently wondered how it would feel to wear only clothes that help me feel like my most authentic self."

"Yeah well you are in a great position to do just that."

"Guess so," she says.

"Plus I'm sure you enjoy summer dresses a lot more than dress pants, right?"

"You have no idea."

"Let's hope not," I say. "I'd look terrible in a summer dress."

"Oh, I think you'd look lovely if you had the right shoes."

"Thanks?"

"You're welcome. I guess I was just looking for permission. You know, validation."

"Permission granted," I say.

"Thanks. I might spend tomorrow getting rid of the non-me clothes."

"Let me know if you need any emotional support when you're jettisoning your pants," I say and then immediately wish I had an undo button for my fumble-prone mouth. "Wait...I could've said that better."

It's nearly two in the morning by the time we finish our meals and discussion. Outside the restaurant, creased off-white clouds look like stretched cotton balls hanging in the night sky, backlit by moonlight. Light snow dusts our shoulders, and my breath steams the air in front of my face as we thank Aili and Julie for their time and their ears. Hugs and goodbyes are exchanged, and then both women walk in the direction opposite ours, two figures shrinking in the distance with each step forward. In a moment they are but indiscernible specs on the concrete horizon, and then they are gone.

By the time we say farewell and then finally trudge into the apartment at which we're staying, I'm ready for sleep. Thankfully, a kind reader is allowing Ryan and me to crash on her livingroom couch and floor. Ryan takes the couch, and the cold hardwood floor is, well, cold and hard and wood, an unkind sleeping surface.

But it's well worth it. Worth it because the message is spreading. Worth it because people who've never even considered the simpler side of life are now asking better questions, seeking better answers, and pursuing contentment outside of material things. Worth it because a few weeks from now, an even larger crowd will attend our final tour stop in Seattle. Worth it because the message keeps spreading.

Amongst the chilled Toronto street noises outside, and my gratitude inside, I welcome the sleep. Cold floor or no, I feel warmth inside.

12 || Rearviews & Windshields

March 2013

"All my shoes are dancing shoes, and the world is my dance floor," Colin Wright says from the passenger-side's backseat. "But sometimes I have to stop dancing." Colin is in the middle of discussing how he declutters his mind, speaking mostly to Ryan, who is picking his nails in the passenger seat.

I'm silent behind the wheel, listening to these two goofballs, the stereo ratcheted all the way down. The road murmurs beneath us, white noise peppered with conversation. The street recedes into the back window as the car propels us forward through a green light. I'm driving slowly, careful to avoid speeding through life—my life—no longer wasting my summers waiting for snow, my winters waiting for sun, taking each season as it comes, appreciating the warmth of the sun, the cleansing of the snow.

"So during this time you just do like *nothing*?" Ryan posits over his shoulder, his brow furrowed.

"Nothing," Colin says.

"Like nothing at all?"

"Nothing at all."

"But my time is too valuable to do nothing. We have only twenty-four hours in a day."

"Obviously."

"So we should use those hours to the best of our ability, shouldn't we?"

"I think what you're saying is that we should always work hard," Colin says,

"Yeah, and do our best to make the most of those hours. Work hard, play hard."

"Cut out the chaff. Increase output. Get things done."

"Exactly," Ryan agrees.

"I tend to agree," Colin pauses and then continues. "And while we both have a propensity for productivity, I think we can be more effective, and more productive, if we take a long twenty-minute pause each day."

Ryan blinks from the passenger seat. Today's sun, a dim aperture amid a ceiling of curled white, is attempting to pierce the thick sky overhead. Great chunklets of snow are falling on the windshield and then whisked away by sporadic wipers.

"I call it my Twenty Minutes of Awesome," Colin says.

"Sounds like a euphemism."

"Hmm. I guess it kind of does, doesn't it? Anyway—"

"So how's it work?"

"The whole idea stems from meditation and yoga and even prayer—those types of body/mind exercises. Except updated for the modern man.

"Or woman," I add.

"Meditation? Sounds a little crunchy to me," Ryan says.

"Maybe," Colin acknowledges. "But it isn't really hippieish or spiritual or whatever. Basically, I take twenty minutes each day to sit quietly, doing nothing with my body. Nothing. No playing computer chess or texting or doodling or reading or watching TV. I just sit or lie awake, alone, smothered in my own thoughts, undisturbed—no phone, no computer, no music—and I just stare off into space, unfocus my eyes and let my mind wander. I find that my mind generally dawdles first to the important items of the day—things like my to-do list, my schedule, projects I'm working on, did I remember to respond to that one email?, et cetera—which is fine."

"So tangents are OK?"

"It doesn't matter what you think about, just that you know you've got some time to think."

"So what's the point?"

"Taking time for ourselves, especially when we're overwhelmed and don't want to, helps declutter the mind. *Everyone* has twenty minutes a day to clear their mental clutter."

"But what do you *do* during those twenty minutes?"

"Use the time however you want—as long as you're doing nothing."

"Huh?"

"If you just need some time to empty your mind and think about nothing, that's perfectly fine. If you want to do mental calculations for your taxes, that's cool too. It's *your* time. Sometimes I'll just let my mind wander in circles. But generally I will first think about my responsibilities, current projects, long- and short-term goals, and the like. Often I'll remember something that I dropped the ball on and need to get to right away, or recall a name or idea I'd been trying to remember while in 'productivity mode' earlier that day. Eventually, though, the thoughts tumble away, and by the end of my twenty minutes, the clutter is cleared, I feel refreshed."

Just a few minutes ago, Ryan and I retrieved Colin from the Greyhound Bus station at the edge of downtown Missoula, Montana. The three of us are going to spend the next six months together in our new HQ here. We are renting a house together here, as well, *Three's Company*-style. We decided it would be prudent to work together in person for a while—to live within the same time zone and settle in to apply our collective noses to the grindstone of the business we've slowly been building for the past eight months: Asymmetrical Press.

Back in the spring of last year, when Ryan and I were plunked in Ohio for a stint, between legs of touring, Colin was traversing the contiguous forty-eight with a beautiful Icelandic girl named Jona, traveling exclusively on Greyhound buses.[94] When their rickety bus stopped on Dayton's west side, a place I rarely have much reason to visit, I scooped them up, and we spent the better part of a week together. Unbeknownst to me, much of our time together consisted of shop talk, during which time Colin approached Ryan and me with a business idea[95]: with everything we'd learned in the blogging world in the past fifteen months, why not share our collective knowledge with the world? Over cups of coffee at Press Coffee Bar,[96] Colin articulated what we already knew: much of the current publishing landscape has changed, and we likely wouldn't've ever "made it" had we relied solely on the old model. But here we were, successful independent publishers, kowtowing to no one.

What's interesting is that I had always been a DIY kind of guy, even in the corporate world, where I climbed the ladder without a college degree or any of the usual qualifications. And now without really intending to be, Ryan and I were successful DIY publishers. We built an audience on our own, and thus didn't have to answer to anyone but ourselves. No gatekeepers, no middlemen, no red tape—just us writing for a large group of attentive readers who find worth in our words.

Enter stage left: Asymmetrical, a publishing company for the indie at heart.[97]

I believe that no author must worship at the altar of the old guard, that writers needn't "submit" to anyone. Anyone can now successfully publish on their own, soup to nuts, controlling every morsel of the process. The present day is the most exciting time in history to be an author. No longer are we beholden to the gatekeepers; no longer must we compromise our craft. For the first time in publishing history, we are in control. I know this first hand. And the three of us aren't just some hacks who write about writing. Nope. Rather, we are a trio of guys who took matters into our own hands; we refused to wait for someone else's permission to publish our work. And guess what: we've been successful. Between the three of us, we've published more than a dozen books (nonfiction, fiction, and memoirs), several of which have been bestsellers; we've toured internationally; and we've established audiences larger than many traditionally published authors.

I don't say this to rag on traditional publishing—they have long done good work, and still do, and many traditional publishers are true advocates for their authors—but the gang and I're giddily excited about the potential that things like ebooks, on-demand printing, and the interconnectivity of social media have brought to the forefront. This is a time of great uncertainty, but uncertain times are when new normals are born. Traditionally published or no, we are entering the age of the Authorpreneur.

For the first eight months of Asymmetrical's existence, we worked on refining our business model, building the brand, and hunting down talented authors from completely different hemispheres.[98] It's no mistake that we named the company

Asymmetrical. Everything we do—from how we approach publishing, to how we deal with distribution—is a little off, askance, a vacation from established and accepted norms. Said another way: as the publishing industry evolves, so must we.

It's been four months since Ryan and I made tracks from Ohio to our mountainside cabin in Montana. After a hundred twenty days of Walden Pond–ish living, we are leaving our remote cabin to write the next chapter of our lifelong story. But we'll still be situated in the Treasure State, seventy-eight miles west, in Missoula, where we will establish our new headquarters.

Why Missoula of all places? Well, we decided to find a nice home somewhere in the US—a place we could work and live and collaborate more easily. For us, this meant more than simply starting a company; we are more interested in creating a lifestyle. Not having lived in the country for almost four years, Colin hoped for a city that was unique of character and alive culturally, while Ryan and I both wanted to find a place full of excited, independent people with a penchant for a high quality of life.

When searching for the right city, what struck all three of us about Missoula was that it has an almost unfairly outsized culture for the number of people who live here. It's a city of people who aren't afraid to shirk traditions if something newer makes more sense, a place where typically dogma-hardened, brittle ideas like politics have a bit more bend to them,[99] and having a massive old truck doesn't mean you're a cowboy, and having a gallery showing off your work doesn't mean that you're not. Missoula is a city of culturally literate pioneers. People get things done, while also appreciating the food, drink, and ideas beyond what they grow in their own backyards.[100] Said another way, Missoula is a very big small town, an asymmetrical city in a state born of asymmetry.

Not to mention its beauty. A college town situated along the

Clark Fork and Bitterroot Rivers at the convergence of five mountain ranges in Big Sky Country, Missoula is, umm, like…just beautiful—like, indescribably beautiful—and is thus an inspiring place to create (it is, after all, the inseparable backdrop to Norman MacLean's classic novella, *A River Runs Through It*). Plus the cost of living here is relatively low, an important factor whenever you're attempting to run a low-overhead business. Not to mention the University of Montana has a solid creative writing program, from which we've found some of our thirty-five passionate interns to work side-by-side as we grow.

In many ways, this move sort of feels like a kind of strange mix of grad school and elementary school.[101]

There are many ways to learn. Many methods and techniques, many ways to acquire new skills, many teachers and mentors from whom we can gain knowledge. One way is often referred to as "continuing education." Graduate schools, trade schools, and various seminars and workshops offer this kind of study. This approach allows one to append his or her existing education, to build atop a firm foundation.[102]

Another way is to start anew. Not unlike kindergarten, this manner of learning is simultaneously terrifying and exciting, because everything in the atmosphere is so new, so vivid, so uncertain and uncharted. Growth happens rapidly amid the terror and excitement of elementary school.[103]

Both learning structures possess their own advantages and disadvantages, obviously. Thankfully, in today's world, we can have a hand in both methods, enjoying the fruits of uncharted territory while building upon the necessary bedrocks of an adult life.

For Ryan and me, our recent move to Missoula with Colin is both elementary school and grad school. We're building on top of a sound structure, a solid, two-year-old foundation,[104] but we're also embracing the uncertainty of a new place with new people,[105] a new business, and new daily practices and routines that will shape our growth in remarkable ways.

Elementary school can be terrifying, but you grow through the fear. Ultimately, you've won when your dreams have broken past your fears.

Eventually, we'll graduate kindergarten. What's new and exciting/terrifying today will soon become routine, just another part of everyday life. When this happens, we'll need to move on to the next elementary-school experience if we want to keep growing. Without growth, people atrophy: we waste away, and in a meaningful way we die inside. Hence, we must continue to find new ways to grow, new elementary schools to crash.

Our new neighborhood is eerily quiet, something I didn't expect from the University District. Our new home's wood floors are creaky, the paint is fresh, and there is more storage space than any of us needs. During our first week in this town, winter's chill is still gripping the air as we find beds for our home and desks and basic office furniture for our new office space just on the other side of the University, about a mile's walk from our house.

When it comes to personal items, it takes me very little time to unpack everything, including my simple red telephone, a home phone I've had for at least a decade. The problem with homes, however, is that once we establish a long-term dwelling, it's easy to accumulate a bunch of junk we don't need. I built my first house when I was twenty-two, a feat that seems ridiculous now, but its size was even more ridiculous.

Too often, we think we have to fill all our space, every corner nook and hidden cranny crammed with supposed adornments. We believe that if a room is nearly empty, then it is underutilized. So we buy stuff—silly stock paintings and decorative thingys and furniture—to fill the void. Ultimately what we're doing is attempting to establish the place in which we live as our *home*, an extension of ourselves. And so the logic goes: the more I buy, the more this place is *my* home.

The problem with this line of thinking is that it's circuitous and never-ending. A home is a home for one reason: we call it home. The stuff doesn't make it *your* home—you do.

Sometimes it helps to have a reminder, though, which means I like to have one thing prominently displayed—just one—something unique that reminds me I'm home. For me, my one thing is a plain red telephone, a relic from my twelve years in the telecom industry. It's a simple, beautiful design that stands out,[106] and whenever I see it, I know I'm home.

For someone else, their red phone could be a one-of-a-kind painting, a photograph, a child's framed drawing. When we have a single reminder of home, everything else begins to look superfluous, even silly.

I am standing in line at my favorite cafe, surrounded by smells and sounds. I've been a Missoulian for maybe six weeks now; my sidekicks and I love it here so far. An uptempo milieu of electric guitar and light percussion is occupying the atmosphere around me, an Andy Davis tune, and I'm singing along—"It's a gooooooood life; it's a good, good life"—like a tone-deaf idiot, missing every-other note, mumbling the words I don't know while looking out the large window to my left, staring into the blankness of the morning. A navy-blue Volkswagen, similar to Colleen's VW, is attempting to park on the snowcovered street outside. It's the first week of spring, but Missoula has yet to receive the memo. Everything outside is blanketed white, so clean and absolute.

I smell coffee. The smell alone is a near-religious experience. The cafe's manager, Jerod, is perched behind a large, shiny espresso machine, manning the military-grade controls, pulling and twisting levers and knobs at precise intervals as the mammoth appliance emits the grinding and wisping sounds associated with good coffee. I imagine Jerod has more than one engineering degree. The whole scene is impressive in the way a kid breakdancing on the street is impressive; it's completely foreign to me, but I'm mesmerized. How could you not be?

People's faces change, visibly brighten, when they enter the cafe's main room, kicking snow from their boots and brushing melted flakes from their parkas. Their postures autocorrect under the high ceilings; the average height of each patron seems to increase at least half an inch as they stand in line, bathed in natural light and coffee aroma.

Jerod makes the best Americanos in Montana—the best. Behind the machine, he's wearing a three-piece suit and a contemplative look that says he's serious about his coffee but somehow simultaneously not so serious that he doesn't know how to have fun. If I tried to affect the same expression, the customers behind me would surely call 911, thinking I was having a mild stroke, but Jerod pulls it off with cool confidence, a professional among professionals, joyed by his labors.

It's my turn to order: Americano, black. The dark-haired girl at the register is wearing a smile I'd like to frame. She's intimidatingly attractive, and so I fumble for something clever to say when she asks me how I'm doing. But I've got nothing, no words: my mouth, a swordless sheath, a book without pages.

I pull out my wallet to pay, peeling a few singles from my thin stack. I don't even consider using my credit card—not anymore at least. The snow keeps calm everything outside the windows, huge flakes like wet chips of white paint peeling off the sky. Cash—not a debit card, but cold hard cash—is the only currency I use these days; it's harder to part with, makes me celebrate over each purchase. Every dollar I let go of is like letting go of one dollar of my freedom. I place a dollar in the jar labeled "tipping is sexy" and smile at the brunette.

But I haven't always been this way (well, I've always smiled at brunettes, but I haven't always been responsible with money).

I'll be thirty-two in a few months, and for the first time in my adult life, I am free of debt. That's a weird thing for me to be able say. You see, from the time I was eighteen—when Chase Bank granted me my first line of credit, a MasterCard with a five thousand dollar limit, which would've made any poor kid from Ohio salivate—until last month, nearly fourteen years later, I've had some sort of debt. As my twenties mounted, so did my tab with the creditors.

First it was just that one credit card, and then, when that one was maxed out, it was two. And then three. Visa, MasterCard, even Discover (American Express wasn't irresponsible enough to grant me a line of credit, not for several years at least).

But that's OK, I was "successful," so I could afford it, right? Unfortunately, I was never great at math. Perhaps I should've financed a calculator before maxing out a half dozen cards.

At twenty-eight, a decade into my accumulation, once my mother started dying, I was forced to look around at all the stuff surrounding me. It was everywhere. My house was full of things I'd purchased in an attempt to find happiness. Each item had brought with it a twinge of excitement at the check-out line, but the thrill always waned shortly after each purchase, and by the time the credit-card statements arrived, I was overwhelmed with guilt, a strange kind of buyer's remorse. And so I'd do it all over again, soaking in the suds of consumption, in search of something that resembled happiness, an elusive concept that got farther and farther away the more I chased it.

Eventually, happiness was just a speck on the horizon, way off in the distance. The closer I got, the farther I had to go. Turns out that I'd been running as fast as I could in the wrong direction. Oops. The stuff wasn't doing its job; it wasn't making me happy. Depression set in when I no longer had time for a life outside of work, laboring eighty hours a week just to pay for the stuff that wasn't making me happy. I didn't have time for anything I wanted to do: no time to write, no time to read, no time to relax, no time for my closest relationships. I didn't even have time to have a cup of coffee with a friend, to listen to his stories. I realized that I didn't control my time, and thus I didn't control my own life. It was a shocking realization.

What I did with that revelation, however, is much more important than the revelation itself. Faced with epiphany, I turned around and started walking—not running—in the right direction. I spent two years living under new spending standards—my Ramen Noodles Meal Plan, slashing all my nonessential wants and likes along the way[107]: I sold the big house (at a significant post-crash loss) and moved into a small apartment; I paid off my car and kept driving it without considering a new one; I cut up the credit cards and started paying for everything with cash; and I bought only the things I needed. Ultimately, I discovered that I truly needed far less than I thought I did. For the first time in my life, I could see happiness getting closer and closer as I walked away from the stuff I thought would make me happy and toward real happiness. My friends and family started noticing my changed demeanor too. Over time, life was calmer, less stressed, simpler.

I spent time paying off debt, incrementally, month by month, bill by bill, getting rid of everything superfluous so I could be less tied to my income, less tied to a job that ate up all my time. It was a long road. It took two laser-focused years to eliminate eighty percent of my debt, and after I walked away from my career, I took a sizable pay cut, but I still focused on paying down the debt, spending two years slapping around that remaining twenty percent, never losing sight of the freedom that hid behind it.

Today I'm seated at a table by the window, sipping an Americano I paid for with cash, thumbing through pages of the *Missoulian* (also paid for with cash). I glance up from the pages periodically, watching the white streets become enveloped by more white. It's like the opposite of a Hitchcock film out there, all hope and promise, a beautiful cleansing. Eventually I see Ryan enter the cafe's doors, a huge, goofy grin on his face, snow caked to his eyebrows, his hair untamed. He looks like he has a good story to tell. I'm waiting to hear it. I've got the time.

Just as he sits down, my phone rings. When I pull it from my pocket, Colleen's photo, with her loopy curls and big blue eyes, overtakes the caller ID. We haven't spoken in months. My heart speeds up as my finger stretches for the green ACCEPT button.

"Hello?"

"Hi. Can we talk?"

Given the standard conventions of storytelling, this chapter is probably supposed to be the part of the book where everything culminates in a crescendo of bliss and benediction—the climax followed by the denouement that ties together all loose ends. But it's not. Real life just isn't structured that way. At least *my* life isn't. My life hasn't followed a traditional story arc. If this book does in fact have a climax, then it likely occurred somewhere around chapter seven. The climax of *my* story, however, is not inside these pages at all. My life will climax somewhere to the right of the frame, many pages beyond the bound and glued front and back covers of this tome. That's real life. My life.

And it's your life too, because you are here as well, have been the whole time, a fly on the wall of my journey, which is to say *our* journey, because in so many ways, we are just the same.

Now I'd like for you to imagine your life a year from now. Two years. Five. Imagine living a healthier life, one in which you don't just look better, you *feel* better. Imagine a life with higher standards. Imagine a life with less clutter, less stuff, fewer distractions. What would it look like? Imagine your life with less—less stress, less debt, less discontent. What would it feel like? Now imagine your life with more—more time, more contribution, more elation. Imagine better, more interesting relationships. Imagine sharing meals and conversations and experiences and smiles with people who have similar interests and values and beliefs as you. Imagine growing with your peer group and your loved ones. Now imagine cultivating your passion until you can't imagine a day without pursuing it. Imagine creating more than you consume. Imagine giving more than you take. Imagine a consistent commitment to growth. Imagine growing toward your limits and then past your limits and waving back with a smile. Imagine still having problems, but *better* problems, problems that fuel your growth and excitement, problems you want to face. Imagine getting everything out of the way so you can love the people closest to you. Imagine the myriad ways you can show your love, not just say it, but really *show* it. Imagine holding hands and exchanging hugs. Imagine making love with the man or woman you love, unencumbered by the trappings of the noisy world around you, fully in the moment, two bodies, flesh and hearts as one. Imagine making your priorities your Real Priorities. Imagine real success. Imagine feeling lighter, freer, happier.

What you're imagining is a meaningful life. Not a perfect life, not even an easy life, but a simple one. There will of course still be hardships and pain and times when slipping back to the old passive world is appealing, but you won't have to. Because the real payoff is worth the struggle. We often attempt to hold tightly the life that has already left us, but when we get rid of life's excess, we discover that we're already perfect, right now, beautiful down to our bone marrow.

Sure, there is wreckage in my rearview, mistakes and bad decisions scattered across the landscape. That's alright by me, though. My failures make up the best parts of me.

And I'm certain there are plenty of blemishes on journey ahead. But that's OK. Life's landscape is filled with peaks and valleys. As we trek from one peak to the next, it's important to find ways to enjoy the walking in between.

I don't know where I'll be a year from now. Two years. Five. Wherever it is, it will be intentional, deliberate, meaningful. Maybe I'll plant roots here in Montana and see what grows. Maybe I'll drive east, back to the Midwest, and rediscover its beauty from a new, more mature perspective. Maybe I'll travel north, across the invisible border into Canada, and experience the mapleleaf life for an era. Maybe I'll head farther west and experience the beaches of California, the waves and the sand and the weather. Or maybe I'll voyage south, *way* south, like, say, Costa Rica, and find something or someone unexpected amongst the mountains. Regardless of where my journey takes me, one thing's for certain: I'm ready for everything that remains.[108]

Endnotes by Ryan Nicodemus

1. Like this one. By the way, I'd like to say hello while you're back here. Thanks for flipping back to visit. As you can see, Joshua has relegated my words and their smaller font to the back of the bus, which is where you will find me for the duration of our journey together, meaning it might be prudent to employ two bookmarks while reading. Whatever you do, though, please don't leave me alone back here. It gets lonely sometimes.

2. And to avoid pissing *on* them as well.

3. When Joshua says "storytelling and conversation" here, I think he's saying that much of the syntax in this book is meant to take on the brain-voice as you get closer to the consciousness of the author/narrator.

While writing this book, we wanted to preserve an oralish, tumbling-words, out-loud feel to the work. Hence, you will sometimes see run-on sentences, passive construction, progressive tenses, unconventional compound contractions, compound conjunctions, compound words that aren't necessarily "real" words (e.g., "livingroom," "peanutbutter," "bumpersticker," "foodbank"), and other intentional grammatical *faux-pas* in the writing. These stylistic devices are used to advance the narrative in a meaningful, more realistic way; they also (hopefully) help sculpt conversational tone of the book.

4. Hi! Sorry, there was traffic.

5. I feel the urge to shout "Silence!" toward no one in particular, but there'd be too much irony in such a command.

6. I think my parents used a similar set of blueprints to build my childhood.

7. I drove by that same duplex not too long ago. It was boarded up and vacant.

8. Ahh, so this is where your OCD began.

9. Ah yes, the American Dream. Happiness: buy stuff, and it will come.

10. One of? Try *the* top. Get it right, Millie.

11. Any man who thinks he is going to work less after getting a promotion is setting himself with a poor expectation, one that will lead to pain and disappointment in the long run.

12. The original Joshua Fields Millburn writings. I bet those'll be worth nothing someday.

13. You're like a modern-day Nancy Drew.

14. Good news for me. I wasn't ready for another blockbuster season of *Ryan & Joshua Move Heavy Things*.

15. *Getting Things Done*. It's just a stupid productivity term from our acronym-filled corporate world.

16. When Joshua called, I thought he wanted help putting together his new "cyborg." You can imagine my disappointment when I arrived only to discover we were constructing a narrow table.

17. Let's be honest: late to the social-media picnic, Joshua signed up for Twitter, Facebook, and, ahem, MySpace all on the same day.

18. Good god, Millie. Man-crush much? Also: sandy-blond? Am I colorblind or did Colin have different color hair back then? I've always thought of his hair as being the color of a sun-dappled patch of freshly turned garden soil.

19. "Sexy, made-for-the-movies lifestyle" are Joshua's words, not Colin's, although they seem to be accurate since both of Colin's memoirs have been optioned by Hollywood production companies to be made into movies.

20. Mind you that by this point only the host and Colin are speaking; the co-host hasn't uttered a single syllable. It appears as if she is either mute or is contractually obligated not to speak.

21. You were still using Yahoo in 2009? Why not just do a DogPile search or AskJeeves!?

22. I've never once witnessed you wearing a hat.

23. Years later, whenever we're on a book tour, it's easy to identify audience members who were experimenting with Project 333: they were always the best-

dressed folks in the room. Simple is the new black indeed. Because simple is always in style, but never trendy.

24. *Popular* might be an understatement. *Zen Habits* is *Time* magazine's number-one blog in the world.

25. It didn't help that you broke a vertebra during our freshman year.

26. I'm not exactly a raving fan of feng shui, but, as a fairly "regular" Midwesterner, a clean room makes for a more productive space to work and a more enjoyable space to live.

27. This is all, of course, not as easy as it sounds. But, then again, it's simpler than you may think. Once we are able to associate enough pain with the flame, we gain enough leverage to make a change.

28. Two women? I simultaneously love and hate this man.

29. Colin + Joshua's first date, how bromantic.

30. Hey, how much does a hipster weigh? One Instagram.

31. You forgot to mention his dreamy blue eyes.

32. It turns out that those are just the most popular blogs.

33. Was I really that big of an asshole during my corporate days?

34. While this conversation certainly did happen, it actually occurred a few days later, when I took Joshua to Subway for a $5 footlong (you're welcome, Millie).

35. Less patient? I prefer to say I'm more "action oriented."

36. Actually, it was Joshua's idea to *pack*, my idea to *party*. I mean come on: if you put the word "party" at the end of anything it's instantly more fun, right?

37. Hey, but I have a cat!

38. There's a dirty joke in there somewhere.

39. Even though I'm not moving. I am, after all, upside down on my mortgage.

40. I thought we agreed to keep that little "detail" out of the book?

41. So what you're saying is that it works a hundred percent of the time, uhh, ninety-seven percent of the time?

42. I really wish you would have changed her name in the book.

43. I spent the next three weeks unpacking only the items I needed, taking time each night to journal the whole experience. The following are select fragments from my twenty-one-day journey:

> Day 1: Last night before I went to bed I unpacked my toothbrush and face wash. I also 'unpacked' my bed and a set of bed sheets and a comforter.

Also: O'Malley's bowls, his food, and one cat toy. (If I'm going to try out this minimalism thing, then so is my cat, damn it!) Then this morning before work I unpacked a towel and a handful of toiletries: shampoo, soap, razor, etc., followed by the basic necessities: a suit, dress shirt, tie, socks, shoes, belt. However, I was shocked that the first three things I unpacked when I returned home after a long day's work was…my couch, television, and Internet. As soon as I got home I peeled the sheets off the couch and TV and then unboxed the wireless modem, plugged it in, and fired it up. It's a little embarrassing that I reach for my pacifiers first. Oh well, at least nobody will ever read this.

Day 2: I woke up this morning and thought, why is there is a weird echo in my condo? I'm not joking. It actually sounds different in here. A strange kind of quiet. The sound of minimalism?

Day 3: So far I've unpacked not nearly as much as I anticipated. A few dishes. A pot and a pan. A handful of kitchen utensils. A couple suits (I now realize how much I dislike wearing a suit to work every day). Some cleaning supplies. What else do I need?

Day 4: Besides the new echo, my condo looks different too. 'Militarily tidy' is the best way I can describe it. Ninety percent of my junk—everything I own—is packed away in one room, and it feels good. I feel anxious too, but, more importantly, I feel less overwhelmed. Maybe it has something to do with that whole feng shui thing.

Day 5: Where the hell is my favorite coffee mug?!!!

Day 6: After taking the nine bags of trash to the curb for the garbage man I drank a glass of water and washed the glass right after using it (this is different for me considering how I'd usually just put it in the dishwasher and then use another glass later when I needed to). This made me realize how lazy I can be. Seriously. It takes my dishwasher about an hour to complete a cycle. If I just washed the dishes myself it would take me about five minutes. Is it worth it, considering I am saving only five minutes by letting my dishwasher do the work for me, not to mention the money it costs to run the actual dishwasher?

Day 7: O'Malley seems to be enjoying his one toy more than he used to, now that it's his only toy.

Day 8: I've hardly touched most of the stuff I packed a week ago. It's sort of weird. I thought I'd be unpacking more than this.

Day 9: Time and money: we often act as if we have more money than time. It's almost a cultural imperative nowadays. It hasn't always been this way though. A couple decades ago most people had less money and more time, and they knew it too. Today the trend has shifted; these days people find themselves with more money than time—or at least more perceived money (vis-a-vis credit cards). The dishwasher from a few days ago is a good example of this phenomenon. A dishwasher provides five minutes of time, which I obviously find more valuable than the money it costs me to run the dishwasher (and the money it cost me to buy the dishwasher). I guess that's one of the things that minimalism is about: reclaiming your time. Time to do whatever. Time to wash dishes, time to snowboard, time to wakeboard (when is the last time I went to Lake Cumberland?), time to help others in need, time to....

Day 10: Today I didn't unpack anything. I think I need to write that again: Today. I. Didn't. Unpack. Anything. Not a thing. Do I already have everything I need?

Day 11: It's getting colder—unpacked one coat.

Day 12: Why haven't I ever stopped and thought about my beliefs—and where they come from? Not the religious beliefs my father forced on me as a child, but all my beliefs in total. The sum of my beliefs. I'm talking about the house we all believe we need, the two-and-a-half children we believe we're supposed to create, the two cars we believe are necessary to live the American Dream. I'm not sure where all mine came from, but I am discovering that many of my beliefs are total bullshit. I'm learning that my condo, all the shit in it, and the boxes I have packed up are not as important as I once believed they were. I have unpacked only like ten or fifteen percent of my belongings up to this point. I'm really surprised because when I first packed everything, I packed a lot of things I truly believed I needed to keep. I believed it deep down. And yet here are the majority of the boxes. Just sitting here. Unpacked. Unused. My journey up to this point has not only opened my eyes to the stuff I have, but I've noticed the other stuff too. My friends. My habits. My job. My condo. My diet. My health. My family. My thoughts.... When it comes to friends, we grow up in a society where image is everything (remember that Sprite commercial) and in order to have a "cool" image we need to hang out with the right people. My teenage sister, for example, is about half my age and is just now attending high school. Like most freshman she has this big worry about who likes her and who doesn't. I hate to sound like my grandpa here, but if I knew then what I know now I wouldn't have been so afraid, and neither would she. She would realize that her beliefs about being cool won't get her through high school, and they won't keep her from making poor decisions. She also believes that she has to do what the other kids do to be accepted. I did too when I was that age and it's pretty sad when I look back at it, because I realize that I let my friends dictate what my habits were (smoking pot, cigarettes, getting drunk, drugs, etc.). And then there are my beliefs about my job.... When I graduated high school I went to work for my dad's little painting/wallpaper business. The idea was for me to take over the family business one day. We worked in countless million dollar homes, and I realized that painting and wallpapering would never allow me to afford any of the homes I worked in. So I left the family business after four years and I got a sales job at Broadspan. As soon as I earned my first commission check I knew I was on my way to making six figures, and I told myself that once I reached that point everything would be OK. I believed everything would be OK. And I believed this for the last seven years just to realize that unless I'm happy with what I have in the present, no amount of money will make me happy. This is my new belief, but after meeting many happy people I know it's the truth. You know what else is true? We construct our own beliefs. Our friends, our habits, our jobs, our happiness is all up to us. We need to choose carefully.

Day 13: It is amazing to realize that we often don't need the things we think we need. And it's equally amazing to think about what the true cost of these things are. The dishwasher from a few days ago is one example (a not-so-great example, but it made me think about my relationship with time/money, which is important). Everything we buy has extra costs associated with it though—and not just the price on the price tag. Our possessions cost us money, which costs us time to earn. And then they cost us more time to take care of (e.g., clean the house, repair your car, clean your furniture, etc.). They take up extra space in our homes, costing us more money because we need to procure extra square footage just to hold all our shit.

Day 14: That electronic gadget I wanted so badly six months ago? The GPS I don't ever use! Before I boxed it up it was probably in a junk drawer or a closet—unused. I haven't thought a single time about unpacking it.

Day 15: That shirt I just 'had to have' last season? Couldn't live without it, right? Well, it's still boxed up.

Day 16: [No entry.]

Day 17: I'm staring at my new car today. It's fancy, it's new, it has all the upgrades. Great, huh? How many more payments do I have left? Just 57 more! At least it has leather seats that warm my ass on my long drive home from my eleven-hour workday—the workday I'm forced to return to tomorrow so I can continue to make those car payments.

Day 18: Today I logged onto Amazon.com and purchased the Pandigital PhotoLink One Touch Scanner that Joshua recommended. I'm going to spend this weekend digitizing everything I can: old paperwork and files, CDs & DVDs, and those boxes of photographs, which I can put in a digital picture frame instead of keep them in three boxes in my garage.

Day 19: Scanning all this stuff, organizing it on my hard drive, is liberating. Plus I know it's all backed up now, which is great because my physical copies, which I'll soon get rid of, were never backed up anywhere.

Day 20: Another day has gone by without unpacking anything. Not a damn thing.

Day 21: This is it. The last day. Eighty percent of my stuff is still in boxes—forgotten. What have I learned? The bottom line: it's all just stuff. And I don't need most of it. But because I own it, that doesn't make me a bad person—it just means that my priorities have been out of whack for a while. If anything, I think this entire process has helped me re-prioritize. It has helped me focus on what's important. It's crazy to see all the stuff that's packed away, stuff I don't ever use. I just don't need them. Besides a handful of seasonal items (this is Ohio after all), I'm getting rid of everything still in those heaps of boxes in my livingroom. All of it. Which makes me realize that maybe with less stuff I don't need the same income, and if I'm not tied to my income, then maybe I could do something different, something I'm passionate about.

44. The cliche ends up being true: the more you have, the more you stand to lose.

45. Being content with mediocrity makes us compromise what we really want out of life, so we settle, opting instead for what's "safe." But settling should be viewed as a bad thing: sea creatures *settle* to the bottom of the ocean when they die, where they stay, settled, dead among all the other dead things.

46. I hate the saying, "Choose a job you love, and you will never work a day in your life," because it's misleading. Pursuing your mission requires lots of in-the-trenches hard work and madman-type dedication.

47. I had this friend in high school. Her parents had all these strict rules, rules that seemed crazy to me as a teenager. For example, if she left her clothes on the floor for longer than a day, her mom would throw them away. Sounds overly strict, doesn't it? Maybe it was. But guess what. She didn't leave clothes on the floor after the first time her favorite jeans hit the trash can.

What if we did the same thing with our lives? What if we held ourselves accountable with our own rules? Our lives are nothing but rules anyway. Unfortunately, most of our rules are disempowering: If I make a million dollars, then I can be happy. If I get this promotion, then I'll work harder. If someone doesn't like me, then I'm going to feel hurt. Too often our rules are just debilitating if-thens. Perhaps it's time to make some new rules. Today. Empowering rules. Rules that will help us grow in the long run, like: If I wake up today, then I'm allowed to be happy. If I exercise today, then I'll feel more confident. If I spend focused time with loved ones today, then I'm contributing in a meaningful way. If I step outside my comfort zone today, then I will grow.

The key, though, is sticking to the rules no matter what. Rain, hail, sleet, or snow, we must adhere to the rules we create. As long as our rules are empowering, we'll always be glad we did.

48. It's a regional thing. A lot of people in Southern Ohio tend to refer to text messaging as *tex-mexing*.

49. (Initiates slow clap.)

50. What's nice is that, let's say you want to have more than six people, you can: I've found that people are more than willing to bring their own plate, the novelty of which tends to make people smile.

51. You can take a photo tour of Joshua's minimalist apartment at themins.com/apartment.

52. Is that why I saw all those caged bunny rabbits at your apartment?

53. Well, not *too* crazy.

54. Like very, very basic.

55. That doesn't count my mom visiting the site once a day, does it?

56. Unless you consider pushing the buttons on the remote control to be work.

57. Amen. I know grown men in their thirties who play video games more than five hours a day.

58. Thankfully Joshua continued to buy hygiene products.

59. It's no coincidence that Josh's average hours per week spent at my house—on *my* laptop—skyrocketed around this time.

60. There's only one way to find out. And while it's frustrating at first, it's an enlightening experience.

61. Now we're always within an arm's—or a *click's*—reach.

62. He's not kidding. In an effort to help me organize my twenties, Joshua sent me a "goals" spreadsheet (literally!), elaborately color-coded and laden with intricate (incomprehensibly complex) formulas.

63. You can find a detailed outline of JFM's diet at themins.com/diet.

64. What if the police are chasing you?

65. Discontent sets in when you start living life for everyone but yourself.

66. After twenty years, you know that punctuality is not my most shining quality.

67. September 29, 2011, was the day I was forcefully nudged toward a more meaningful life. I sat down in the harshly lit conference room and slid a birthday present across the table. It was my boss's birthday. It was less than a month before my own thirtieth birthday. It was also the day I lost my job.

My boss, my boss's boss, and a woman from human resources were sitting on the other side of the large, meticulously polished conference table. My boss shook his head and a frown materialized on his face. I knew it wasn't good news—sitting in a room with your boss, his boss, and HR typically isn't a recipe for optimism—but my first thought was, I*t really sucks for him that he has to let me go on his birthday.*

"We've eliminated your position with the latest round of cuts. This change is effective immediately," the HR woman said. And that's when everything changed.

Seven months after Joshua left his job, I was laid off with no notice, with no friendly warning, with no heads-up—just blind-sided after working incredibly hard for a corporation. Seven years, eight job titles, living the Corporate Dream—over in an instant.

"Do you have any additional questions before HR goes over the details with you?" my boss asked.

No, I didn't have any additional questions. I just sat there and thought, *This is the best thing that could have happened to me.*

It was as if a gigantic weight had been lifted off my shoulders. I hadn't been happy for I while; I knew it was time for me to move on, and this was the nudge I needed to jump off Corporate America's cliff…ahem, I mean ladder.

It was the nudge I needed to focus full-time on my passions, the nudge I needed to focus my time on the important things in life—my health, my relationships, my growth as an individual, and contributing to other people in meaningful ways. This is the drastic change I needed.

Thankfully, my gradual transition into minimalism has allowed me to purchase less stuff, spend less money, cut most of my bills, payoff most of my debt, save a little money, and live with less.

Of course, I'll still need to make other cutbacks: I contacted a realtor to help sell my condo. I'm also attempting to sell my car. But none of that matters in the grand scheme of things—I'm free!

I'm excited to focus on something I'm passionate about. For as long as I can remember, even when I was a teenager with a handful of younger siblings, mentoring has been my passion. Mentoring was also the most enjoyable aspect of my corporate career. Unfortunately, a lot of things occurred in the corporate world that prevented me from allocating much of my time to that passion.

But thanks to the success of *The Minimalists*, I'll be able to do what I love. Although I'll my make significantly less money, I'll be able to mentor people online and not have to worry about finding another corporate job.

Even more important, I'll have more time for the people I love. This has been a huge struggle for me ever since I started my corporate climb. As I advanced my career and climbed the corporate ladder, I often worked sixty or seventy hours a week, and I lost track of family and close friends. I started to feel like my job was more important than my relationships. I believed they would understand why I wasn't around as much. And some people did understand, but it didn't feel good. It didn't feel right. We can't just brush off our friends and family and expect to feel fulfilled.

I feel a kind of post-layoff joy, but I'm not going to lie, I also feel fear from this transition. I'm not going to let that fear prevent me from living meaningfully, though. No, I don't think you need to leave your job to live a meaningful life; but, for me, it was the nudge I needed to get the balance back in my life.

For those of you who may be facing a similar situation (maybe you're uncertain about your job or you're unsure whether you should go pursue your passions), you might be looking for advice. Well, I don't have all the answers, but what I do have is my commitment to add value whenever I can. So feel free to shoot me an email—RN@themins.com—and maybe I can help point you in the right direction.

68. Yeah, if you knew the names of any of those constellations.

69. Well, that could certainly be misconstrued.

70. A town some locals refer to as "G. Vegas" sarcastically because of its too many, too bright, too ugly neon lights.

71. I've always loved Colleen's frequent, liberal use of curse words.

72. Hence, another platitude ends up being true: giving is living.

73. Johnnie Walker isn't exactly piss.

74. Twice.

75. That's the last time I force you to eat gluten.

76. Well, Joshua has, likely because he looks much too much like a young Christopher Walken.

77. Unbelievable but completely true.

78. Also true. In fact, you can follow our fake band, Love by Proxy, on Twitter: @LoveByProxy.

79. Yikes!

80. Most notably, idiotic stickers involving different "creative" uses of the Confederate Flag.

81. Ahem, our "tour bus" is actually just my decade-old Toyota Corolla.

82. No kidding: even when it snows, which it does a lot during wintertime, it's stubbornly sunny outside.

83. Wasn't it the Unabomber (not Thoreau) who moved to a cabin in the-middle-of-nowhere Montana?

84. Besides, unlike Thoreau we have Wi-Fi. Now, granted, we had to convince the local telephone company to run a line to the cabin (the original line had long since been cut). Thankfully we'd worked in the telecom industry for a while, so we knew who to talk to and how to get it done, a somewhat impressive feat for a place that even the U.S. Postal Service doesn't deliver to. Which, on a somewhat related note, also means we had to get a P.O. Box and drive to town to pick up our mail.

85. The book you're reading right now.

86. You can take a photo-tour of our cabin at themins.com/cabin.

87. Have you been peeing in our shower?

88. Mel, short for *Melissa*, although an utterly different Melissa from the Melissa briefly mentioned in Chapter 6.

89. And, umm, metaphorically, I hope.

90. Shouldn't it be the Canadian Dream? Just saying.

91. By September, the workload of filtering the interview requests and tour scheduling and the like was too much for us amateurs to handle, so we hired Sarah Miniaci, our wonderfully talented, supremely focused, and incredibly photogenic PR agent.

92. That's not true: I've seen you pick up a hammer dozens of times…and then hand it to me.

93. Millie had a water with lemon. I guess that counts as a "drink."

94. Jona's only experience in America had been a childhood trip to Disneyland, so Colin said he wanted to show her "the real America."

95. A business idea? It was more like a confusing-as-hell, hand-drawn infographic.

96. Which is, by the way, the best coffeehouse in the country. Joshua wrote an essay about it at themins.com/coffee

97. If you're interested, you can learn more about Asymmetrical at www.asymmetrical.co/about.

98. See www.asymmetrical.co/authors for more info.

99. During our first week in town, a gun-toting lesbian couple invited us over to eat the elk they'd recently hunted. Both women were vegetarians, as are Joshua and I, which meant there was plenty of elk for Colin.

100. Missoula is a place in which the best burrito in town is served at a pizza parlor.

101. And not just because of our lame, adolescent jokes.

102. Or a shoddy foundation.

103. Both emotions—terror and excitement—tend to conjure the same physiological reactions: rapid heartbeat, dilated pupils, sweaty palms; this type of attentiveness significantly aids personal growth.

104. It's hard to believe it's been more than two years since we started TheMinimalists.com. Strangely, it's also hard to believe that it's been only two years since we started. It's all been so fast, yet so much has happened during these past two years.

105. Random observation: roughly every third girl in Missoula seems to be named either Katie or Kate or Kathryn. Kathleen and KT and Kat and other derivatives are also common. I have no idea what this means.

106. Very true. The same phone is on display in the MoMA.

107. Read about JFM's need/want/like list at www.themins.com/want.

108. I guess sometimes the ending isn't really the end.

Made in the USA
Charleston, SC
25 October 2013